TAP THE SUN

Passive Solar Techniques and Home Designs

CMHC offers a wide range of housing-related information.
For details, contact your local CMHC office or call 1-800-668-2642.

Cette publication est aussi disponible en français sous le titre :
CAPTER LE SOLEIL : Techniques solaires passives et modèles de maisons (LNH 2001)

The information contained in this publication represents current research results available to CMHC, and has been reviewed by a wide spectrum of experts in the housing industry. The Corporation, however, assumes no liability for any damage, injury or expense that may be incurred or suffered as a result of the use of this publication or the CD-ROM.

Canadian Cataloguing in Publication Data

Main entry under title:

Tap the sun : passive solar techniques and home designs

2nd ed.
Originally published: Passive solar house designs for Canada/
Allen Associates and Marbek Resources Consultants, c1989.
Issued also in French under title: Capter le soleil.
Accompanied by a CD-ROM.
ISBN 0-660-17267-4
CCG Cat. No. NH15-190/1997E

1. Solar energy—Passive systems. 2. Solar houses—Canada—Designs and plans. I. Canada Mortgage and Housing Corporation. II. Title. III. Title: Passive solar house designs for Canada.

TH7414.T36 1997   690.8370472   C97-980478-7

Revised and reprinted: 1998
Printed in Canada

Produced by CMHC

ACKNOWLEDGEMENTS

Many knowledgeable and talented people have contributed to the creation of this book, from its inception through to this second edition. They include the designers and builders who conceived and provided the house designs for the first and second editions: Allen-Drerup-White; IBI Group; Charles Simon; Stephen Carpenter; Snider Reichard & March; John Hix; Richard Kadulski; Barry Hobin; William McCreery; John Carroll and the Manitoba Home Builders' Association.

The research for the material was done by Building Engineering Group, Enermodal Engineering, Leslie Jones and Associates, Ken Cooper, Richard Kadulski, Chris Mattock, Wil Mayhew, Roger Henry and Fanis Grammenos. Wayne Webster, Jim White, Chris Ives and Tom Livingston provided invaluable advice about the content.

The text of the second edition was written by Leslie Jones, with technical and editing assistance from Fanis Grammenos and Roger Henry.

Thanks also go to the graphic designers who gave the book its look and to the project management team from the two collaborating federal agencies — Canada Mortgage and Housing Corporation and Natural Resources Canada.

The photos were provided by Reg Morrison of the Department of Natural Resources of Nova Scotia and CANMET, Natural Resources Canada.

The second edition of the book was jointly funded by Canada Mortgage and Housing Corporation and CANMET, Natural Resources Canada.

CONTENTS

Introduction

Part 1 : Elements of passive solar design

Part 2 : Design Integration and Strategies

Part 3 : Selected House Designs

APPENDICES

INDEX

INTRODUCTION

In most industrialized countries, people are increasingly choosing to live in harmony with nature. In Canada, this trend is known as Healthy Housing. Healthy Housing is Canada Mortgage and Housing Corporation's (CMHC's) vision of housing that promotes the health of its occupants, while protecting the environment and preserving our natural resources.

Healthy Housing is based on five key themes:

• promoting occupant health;
• enhancing energy efficiency;
• improving the efficient use of natural resources;
• encouraging environmental responsibility; and
• being affordable for everyone.

The interest in Healthy Housing has come about largely in response to the need for healthy indoor environments and housing development that does not deplete or damage the earth's resources. In Canada, a major portion of our energy consumption occurs in buildings. Compared with other countries, our buildings consume proportionately more energy because of our harsh climate and relatively low fuel costs. Residential buildings alone account for 20 percent of Canada's gross energy use and contribute a similar percentage to the nation's greenhouse gases.

Our modern heating and cooling systems have enabled architects and builders to create comfortable interior spaces, independent of the external climate and building shell design. Despite enormous regional differences in climate, it is the similarity of our buildings, not their differences, that is surprising. Yet, buildings that provide an artificially modulated indoor climate too often cause health problems for their occupants, particularly people who are susceptible to allergies and illness caused by unhealthy indoor air. Healthy Housing addresses this problem by promoting homes that contribute to both the health of the environment and the people who live in them.

One of the basic building blocks of Healthy Housing is the use of solar energy. The sun is the earth's greatest source of renewable energy—a massive generator that produces more than enough energy to heat all our dwellings. Solar energy is clean, non-polluting and readily available.

Using the sun to heat and light our homes is not a new idea. But the initial thrust, which was prompted by the oil embargo of the 1970s, has now matured, giving us a greater understanding of building science and a range of economical building products not dreamed of 30 years ago.

Canada is a global leader in energy-efficient housing, and our technology is exhibited in countries around the world. For example, Canada was instrumental in dramatically improving window glazing. The first important step occurred centuries ago when glass was placed over an opening in the wall. The next was the development of window systems that were comparable to insulated walls in terms of thermal performance.

Today, a renewed understanding of the environment, of the seasonal variations of solar radiation and the relationship between solar radiation and temperature can lead to housing that achieves comfort through natural processes. The purpose of this book is to promote that objective.

Passive Solar Design

The goal of passive solar design is to collect and use energy from the sun to reduce the consumption of purchased energy while maintaining a comfortable, healthy and pleasing environment. Solar energy is not an alternative to other strategies, such as energy conservation and energy-efficient heating systems, but a complement to them. Designing with sunlight also creates brighter, more interesting interior spaces, and large windows, skylights and solariums are great selling features. However, careful attention to the principles of passive solar design is required to prevent overheating, excessive air conditioning, discomfort near glass and condensation on window panes.

About This Book

The purpose of this book is to help you make the best use the sun's energy in your home. While much of the book contains information of interest to house designers and builders, homeowners will also find it valuable for its practical tips and as a primer on solar energy in general. This audience will find the summaries at the end of each chapter particularly useful.

The book is divided into three parts. Part 1 is an overview of the basic elements of passive solar design. Chapter 1 considers the availability of solar radiation as a resource and relates this resource to our Canadian climate. Chapter 2 explains how solar energy is collected and examines the important role of windows. Chapter 3 describes how solar energy is stored and distributed throughout the house for maximum comfort. Chapter 4 explains how to control summer heat gains by using shading and ventilation strategies. Chapter 5 returns to the subject of windows and looks at a range of supplementary issues, including different types of windows and their effects on thermal comfort and daylighting.

Part 2 brings all the elements together. Chapter 6 explains how to integrate the elements of passive solar heating with other design considerations, and how to evaluate passive solar designs using computer modelling. Chapter 7 discusses site planning and strategies for designing detached, semidetached and row housing. Chapter 8 defines the concept of occupant comfort and sets out guidelines to help achieve the balance of strategies required to create it. To assist the designer, instructions for using the *Comfort Design Checker* software are included in Appendix 2.

Finally, Part 3 presents 20 house designs that use the sun to minimize their energy consumption. These designs all have envelope characteristics that meet or surpass the requirements of the 1995 National Energy Code for Houses (NECH). They were developed by Canadian architects and designers for specific Canadian cities. While each design makes deliberate use of the sun's energy to provide heat, it also meets a variety of needs, desires and budgets. The plans can be used "as is," modified or simply viewed as ideas to help inspire new ways to design with sunlight.

Part 1
Elements of Passive Solar Design

A solar home can be attractive, comfortable and luxurious. It uses the sun's energy for heating and lighting and reduces the need for purchased fuel. But improperly designed, a solar house can be uncomfortable as a result of glare or extreme temperatures. It could even increase fuel bills. That is why it's important to understand the principles of passive solar design when designing, building or choosing a solar home.

Passive solar design focuses on collecting, storing and distributing the sun's heat to maximize its use. Part 1 of this book explains the basic elements of passive solar design and considers strategies for applying these principles.

1 Solar Radiation—the Resource

This chapter explains the basic scientific principles of passive solar heating and describes the components that can improve the performance of a solar home.

In passive solar design, two key considerations are the amount of solar energy collected and the proportion of the home's heating requirements it can provide. These are determined by the sun's intensity and the total seasonal solar radiation for the region, which depend on the latitude and climate at the site location for the house.

Solar Intensity

Above the earth's atmosphere, the intensity of solar radiation has a fixed value of 1,350 W/m² (watts per square metre). But the earth's atmosphere scatters and absorbs the sun's rays causing less solar energy to reach the surface of the earth. Solar radiation achieves its peak intensity at noon and is greatest at the spring equinox (around March 21). In Canada, peak intensity is quite consistent; it varies less than 5 percent, from 957 W/m² at 45°N latitude to 914 W/m² at 53°N latitude.

Other factors affecting the amount of solar energy that reaches the earth's surface are cloud cover and air pollution. On overcast days, while still considerable as a source of heat, solar radiation can be as little as one third of what it is under clear conditions. (See Figure 1.1.)

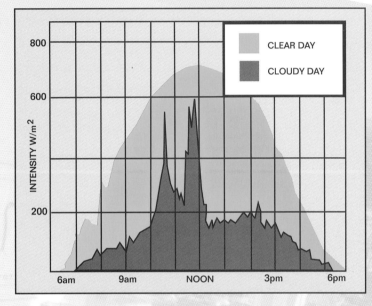

Figure 1.1 Total solar radiation (W/m²) on horizontal surface

Values are for a horizontal surface for typical clear and largely cloudy days around the time of the equinox

Because the sun's rays are scattered as they pass through the atmosphere, they reach the earth as a mix of direct and diffuse radiation. On a clear day, about one fifth of the solar radiation falling on a horizontal surface is diffuse radiation. On an overcast day, all the radiation is diffuse.

Direct radiation is unidirectional. Its intensity is greatest on a surface that is perpendicular to the sun's rays and decreases as the surface is tilted away (i.e., as the angle of incidence (ß) in Figure 1.2 increases). Direct radiation provides the greatest amount of usable heat. Diffuse radiation, on the other hand, is non-directional—its intensity is equal in all directions. Diffuse sunlight on an overcast day and sunlight reflected from snow on the ground can also provide a good deal of heat and serve as a source of glare-free daylight.

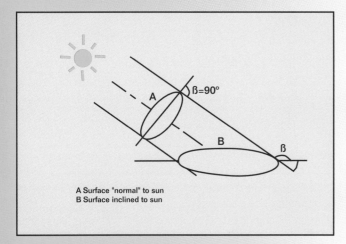

A Surface "normal" to sun
B Surface inclined to sun

FIGURE 1.2 Variation of intensity of direct radiation with surface inclination

A and B receive the same absolute value of radiation (watts), but the area of A is smaller than B and therefore has greater intensity (W/m²)

Incident Solar Radiation

A window's orientation and slope combined with local weather patterns determine how much solar energy it will receive. Figure 1.3 shows the monthly variation in incident solar radiation under clear skies for various window orientations. The graph illustrates:

• Why south-facing windows are best for passive solar heating. (They receive the most heat during the winter when the sun is low.) A south-facing, tilted window receives the most heat in the summer and should be avoided except in sunspaces.

• Why north-facing windows should be avoided. (They receive little heat with peaks in the summer.)

• Why horizontal windows should be avoided. (They receive little heat in the winter and high heat in summer.)

• Why east- and west-facing windows should be kept to a minimum. (They receive little heat in winter with peaks in the summer.)

The variation in the amount of incident radiation is mainly the result of the sun being low in the sky in the winter and high in the summer, as well as low in the mornings and afternoons and high at noon.

The values given in Figure 1.3 include radiation reflected from a ground surface with a reflectance of 20 percent, which is typical of an asphalt driveway. With fresh snow cover, radiation values for vertical surfaces would be approximately 20 percent higher than shown. (Fresh snow cover has a reflectance of about 74 percent.) This variation suggests that driveways or other areas without snow cover should not be located in front of solar-collecting glazing. Figure 1.4 shows a lower range of incident solar radiation resulting from cloudy conditions for a city with a moderately sunny climate. This is the actual amount on which the design will be based.

Climate Variations and Solar Contribution

Passive solar design is the art of balancing solar heat gains and a building's heat losses to achieve the best performance. Therefore, local climate is an

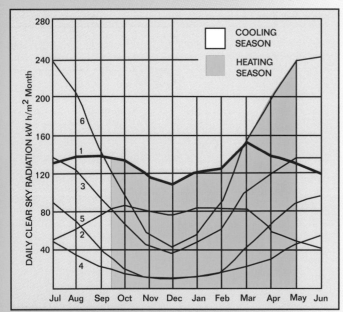

FIGURE 1.3 Monthly variation of solar radiation under clear sky (kW h/m² month) at 45°N latitude

1 to 5 vertical surfaces:

1. South facing
2. Northeast and northwest facing
3. East-west facing
4. North facing
5. Southeast and southwest facing
6. Horizontal surface

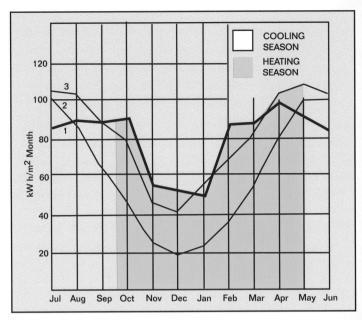

FIGURE 1.4 Monthly variation of incident solar radiation (kW h/m² month) on a vertical surface in Ottawa

1. South facing
2. East facing
3. Southeast facing

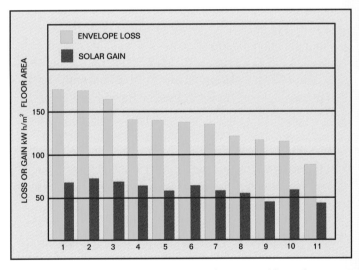

FIGURE 1.5 Relative magnitudes of seasonal heat losses and solar gains kW h/m² for a range of Canadian cities

1. Edmonton	7 . Charlottetown
2. Winnipeg	8 . Toronto
3. Swift Current	9 . St. John's
4. Ottawa	10. Halifax
5. Montréal	11. Vancouver
6. Fredericton	

important factor in the effective use of solar energy. For example, a window in Winnipeg may provide 60 percent more solar energy over a heating season than the same window in Vancouver, even though Winnipeg winters are twice as cold. To understand why, it is necessary to consider other factors, such as insulation levels and the type of glazing.

Figure 1.5 gives the expected solar heat gains and heat losses for an identical house in 11 Canadian cities. It shows that in Canada's more temperate locations, such as Vancouver and Halifax, sun-generated heat can cover a greater proportion of heat losses than in colder areas. It also shows that in cold, sunny climates, like Edmonton and Winnipeg, more solar energy can be made available for heating.

Canada is a better place than many other countries for passive solar heating because the climate is mainly sunny and cold. (See Figure 1.6.) In fact, a well-designed house in Canada can get from one third to almost one half of its heating needs from the sun.

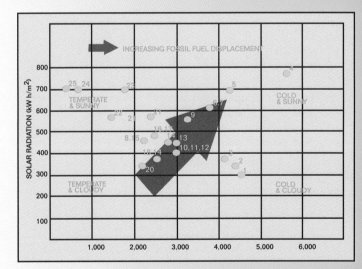

FIGURE 1.6 Comparison of climatic factors of selected countries' radiation values are on a vertical south face over a seven-month heating season

Scandinavia 1, 2, 3
Canada 4, 5, 6, 7, 8
United States 9
Central Europe 10, 11, 12, 13, 14, 15, 16, 17, 18, 19, 20
Australia and Japan 21, 22, 23, 24, 25

Spectral Composition of Solar Radiation

Solar energy is made up of electromagnetic radiation of various wavelengths. As Figure 1.7 illustrates, most of this energy is concentrated in wavelengths between 300 nm (nanometres) and 1,500 nm, with a peak around 500 nm. Near infrared radiation provides useful heat. Visible radiation provides both heat and light that becomes heat when absorbed by room surfaces. Ultraviolet radiation, the part of the solar spectrum which is responsible for sunburn, is almost completely blocked by all types of windows.

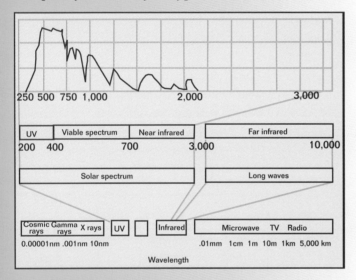

FIGURE 1.7 The electromagnetic spectrum

km = kilometres   mm = millimetres
m = metres   nm = nanometres
cm = centimetres

The composition of the solar spectrum forms the basis for the design of new types of windows whose transmission characteristics vary with different wavelengths. Chapter 2 discusses the rates of transmission for selected types of glass in more detail.

Long waves, although not part of the solar spectrum, are also important in passive solar heating. At normal temperatures, all objects exchange heat through long-wave radiation, and this influences the amount of heat lost through windows.

Daylight

A house design that makes good use of daylight should not need to use electricity for lighting.

Daylight also improves the home's illumination. For daylighting of interior spaces, designers work with the visible portion of the solar spectrum. The quantity of daylight is referred to as illuminance and expressed in terms of lux (lx). It has a direct component called sun illuminance and a diffuse component called sky illuminance.

Sky illuminance is more important than sun illuminance because it can provide natural light in rooms of all orientations throughout the day. The illuminance of the sky at noon on an overcast day in December is around 8,000 lx. A satisfactory lighting level for most domestic chores is 100 lx, and 300 lx is suitable for reading.

Summary

• The two key factors to consider in designing a passive solar home are solar intensity and the total seasonal solar radiation for the area.

• Solar radiation includes direct, diffuse and reflected components. Windows collect solar radiation and contribute significantly to a home's energy needs, even on overcast days.

• South-facing glazing is best for passive solar heating because southerly exposures receive the most sunlight in winter.

• Passive solar design is the art of balancing a building's solar gains against its heat losses. Since solar gains and heat losses vary by geographic area, house designs will vary in different parts of the country.

• Cold, sunny climates offer the greatest potential for solar heating. A well-designed house in Canada can get from one third to one half of its heating needs from the sun.

• Solar radiation ranges from near infrared to ultraviolet wavelengths that include the visible light spectrum. The transmission characteristics of new types of windows vary with different wavelengths.

• A solar house that makes the best use of daylight should need less electricity for lighting.

2. Solar Energy Collection and Window Performance

Chapter 1 examined the sun as a source of energy. It explained the significance of solar intensity and incident solar radiation and stressed the link between local climate and the amount of solar energy available. It also described the spectral composition of solar radiation. Chapter 2 now describes how to gather this resource, the key role played by windows and their energy transmission characteristics.

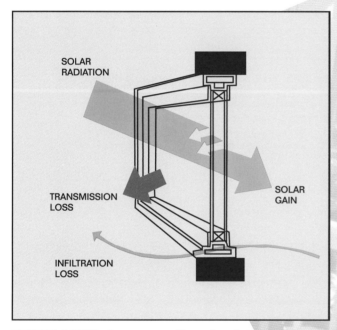

FIGURE 1.8 Window energy flows in winter

The sun's rays entering a house through windows and walls can reduce its heating requirements. However, in well-insulated houses, the solar gains resulting from the transmission of heat through walls is negligible. Windows, on the other hand, are the single most important component in a passive solar house because solar radiation passes directly through transparent glazing.

Glass that admits solar radiation directly to the house is a poor insulator. An insulated wall, for example, might have a thermal resistance (RSI) of about 3.5 while a normal double-glazed window has an RSI value of 0.35—10 times less than the wall. In order to provide a net heat gain, a window must admit more heat than it loses over the heating season.

While advances in technology make it possible to make liberal use of windows to collect heat, understanding how a window performs is important for effective solar heating.

Figure 1.8 shows the energy flows through a window in winter. The relative magnitudes of these energy flows determine whether the window is a net energy provider. While solar gain varies with the intensity and direction of the sun's rays, heat losses due to transmission and infiltration vary with the temperature of the outside air and wind.

The following section examines the major factors affecting these energy flows as well as techniques for ensuring a net positive effect.

Solar Heat Gains

In addition to the types of glass used, there are two other key factors that determine the amount of solar radiation transmitted through glazing: (i) the angle of incidence; and (ii) the number of panes of glazing material.

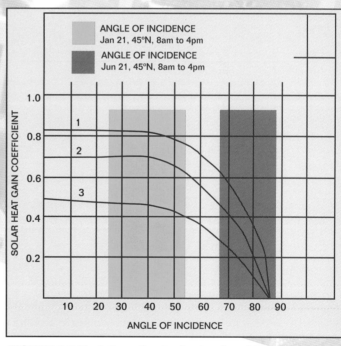

FIGURE 1.9 Variation of solar heat gain with angle of incident radiation

1. Single clear glass
2. Double clear glass
3. Double low-e

Angle of incidence: The angle of incidence is the angle at which the sun's rays strike the surface of the glass. Most radiation is admitted when the angle of incidence is 90°. Up to 50° from perpendicular, the transmission is almost uniform. At 60° from perpendicular, double-pane clear glazing transmits about 20 percent less solar radiation. At 80° from perpendicular, transmission drops by 70 percent.

In winter, the angle of incidence on south-facing glazing is usually less than 50°; in summer, it is most often greater than 50°. (See Figure 1.9.) Therefore, south-facing glazing transmits more solar radiation in winter than in summer—a desirable effect in passive solar design.

In addition, the uniformity of transmission up to 50° provides for flexibility in siting a house. Up to 30° off due south, the amount of solar energy collected stays practically the same. This makes it possible to avoid accidental shading and to take advantage of views. The variation of solar gain with the angle of incidence and the variation

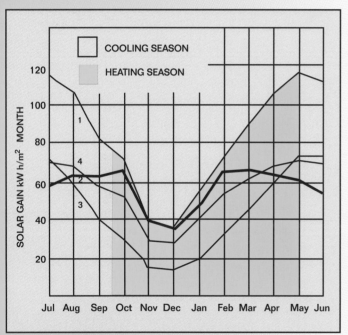

FIGURE 1.10 Typical monthly variation of solar gains (kW h/m² month) through clear insulating glass in Ottawa

1. 45° tilt south-facing
2. Vertical south-facing
3. Vertical east-facing
4. Vertical southeast-facing

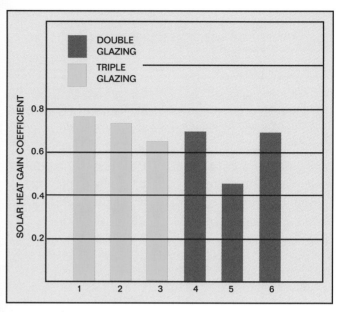

FIGURE 1.11 SHGCs for a range of glass types

1, 4. Air-fill, clear glass
2.   Hard-coat, low-e (e = 0.2)
3, 5. Soft-coat, low-e (e = 0.1)
6.   Suspended low-e film in double glazing

of solar intensity with orientation combine to produce a pattern of heat gains through windows like the one shown in Figure 1.10.

Solar Heat Gain Coefficient (SHGC): The characteristics of a window influence the amount of solar radiation it transmits. These characteristics are expressed by the SHGC. The SHGC is equal to the ratio of solar heat gain to the amount of radiation falling on the window.

When looking at a window's SHGC value, it is important to know whether it applies to the glazing or to the complete assembly (i.e., the glass plus the frame). If it applies to the whole unit, small windows will have lower SHGCs due to the thickness of the window frame. The thinner the window frame, the higher the SHGC and the better the window performs as a solar energy collector. Figure 1.11 gives the SHGCs for a range of glass types. (Figure 1.12 gives the SHGCs for window assemblies.)

Selecting Glazing Size

How much glass area is enough to provide comfort without overheating? The rule for deciding the amount of glazing says that in most areas of Canada, the area of south-facing glass should be between 6 and 10 percent of the heated floor area. This provides a good starting point for design. It assumes that there is adequate air circulation to distribute the solar heat gains and that the thermal storage is limited to the conventional building materials. Materials with greater thermal storage capacity would allow larger windows and more effective use of solar radiation for heating. (See Chapter 8 and Appendix 2 for more information on passive solar strategies for achieving occupant comfort.)

Glazing Materials

The type of glazing material also influences solar heat gain. Not all types of glazing transmit all wavelengths equally well. For example, normal clear glass admits little ultraviolet light (which is why we don't get a suntan through a window) and does not fully admit long-wave radiation.

Figure 1.13 shows the typical transmittance characteristics of various types of glass. The graph appears to indicate that low-emissivity (low-e) glass has poor heat gain properties because it cuts out more than half of the equivalent clear-glass spectrum. However, the portion of the spectrum that it does admit, particularly below 750 mm, carries most of the solar energy. (See Figure 1.7.) Modern glazing materials are available with a wide range of transmission characteristics, including long-wave reflecting, low-iron, solar reflecting, combined solar and short-wave reflecting and tinted.

Long-wave reflecting: Long-wave reflecting, low-e glazing is available in multiple-pane units. The low-e coating is applied to one or more of the internal glass surfaces or added to one or more polyester films mounted between the layers of glass. The coating helps the glass reduce long-wave radiation loss from interior spaces but has little effect on solar heat gain and daylighting.

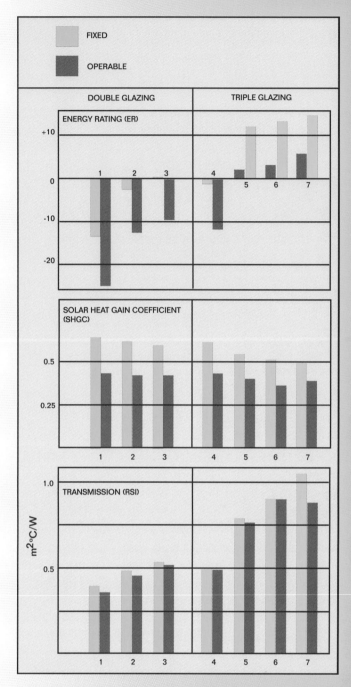

FIGURE 1.12 Typical window assembly ER, SHGC and RSI values

Double Glazing:

1. Air-fill, vinyl-frame
2. Air-fill, low-e, vinyl-frame
3. Low-e, argon-fill, vinyl-frame
4. Air-fill, wood-frame

Triple Glazing:

5. Low-e, argon-fill, foam-filled, vinyl-frame insulated spacer
6. Low-e, argon-fill, foam-filled, vinyl-frame insulated spacer
7. Low-e, argon-fill, fibreglass-frame insulated spacer

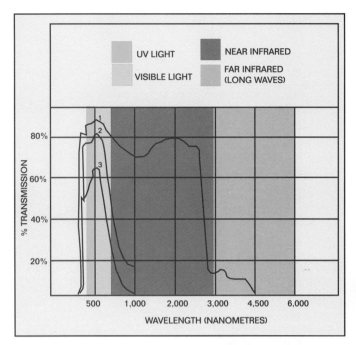

FIGURE 1.13 Selective transmission characteristics of double-glazing units

1. Clear
2. Low-e
3. Low-e, solar-reflecting

Low-e coatings come in two general types: hard coatings and soft coatings. Hard coatings tend to have a higher emissivity than soft coatings and, therefore, are less effective in reducing heat loss. They also have a higher SHGC than soft coatings, which allows more solar heat gain. (See Figure 1.11.) Overall, because of many intervening factors, the best way to choose glazing is by the window energy rating (ER). (See page 14.)

Another factor determining a window's performance is the location of the coating. For residential use in northern climates, the coating is normally applied on the air-gap side of the inside window-pane. This gives the highest SHGC and thermal resistance.

Windows with the right low-e coatings are an excellent choice for passive solar homes because the relatively small drop in solar heat gain is more than offset by the reduction of heat losses through long-wave transmission.

Low-iron: Low-iron glass is tempered glass with less iron in it. This increases its capacity to transmit solar energy. When used instead of regular glass, low-iron glass results in a higher SHGC without any drop in insulation value. For example, double air-filled units can give a 9 percent improvement in SHGC, a desirable increase for passive solar applications. Availability and cost have limited its use in window glass.

Solar-reflecting: Solar-reflecting glazing has a mirror-like appearance and is most commonly used in commercial buildings to limit air conditioning loads. Because its primary purpose is to reduce solar gains, it is unsuitable for passive solar applications.

Combined solar and short-wave reflecting: Some glazings combine solar-reflecting and low-e characteristics. One disadvantage of this in a cold climate is the loss of potential solar heat gain. These windows could reduce overheating in house designs with large areas of east- or west-facing windows.

Tinted: Tinting reduces solar heat gain and the transmission of daylight. It is not suitable for passive solar applications.

Advanced Glazing Materials

In pursuit of better thermal performance, researchers are developing new glazing materials. Some materials that have potential in passive solar design are evacuated glazing, aerogel and switchable glazing.

Evacuated glazing: Evacuated glazing relies on the creation of a vacuum between the panes of glass. Prototype double-glazing units with a very low-e coating have reached a centre-of-glass RSI of 1.76—almost three times as high as a double, low-e, air-filled window. However, when mounted in a frame, their RSI values are not much higher than commercially available high-performance windows due to conduction heat losses around the frame.

Aerogel: Aerogel material combines high thermal resistance with light transmittance of about 65 percent. These characteristics make aerogel virtually "transparent insulation." In windows, aerogel can be used between layers of glass. When a partial vacuum is introduced between the layers, it increases the insulating value significantly. Used as fill for double glazing, aerogel can obtain thermal resistance in the range RSI 1.0-2.0. Its first application could be in skylights or clerestories where its slight opacity would not be a problem.

Switchable glazing: Thermochromism, photochromism and electrochromism are processes by which heat, light and electrical voltage, respectively, can modify the transmission characteristics of glass. Most research and development for building applications focuses on electrochromic systems that can be switched on or off with a small electric voltage. There are windows available that reduce visible light transmission in their switched state, providing privacy and protection from the glare of the sky or the sun. However, they are of questionable value in passive solar applications.

Transmission Losses

Countering the heat gain from the sun, heat flows constantly outward through the windows. Windows lose heat by a combination of radiation, convection and conduction. (See Figure 1.14.)

Radiative heat loss is the most important of these three modes. It accounts for two thirds of the overall heat loss in conventional insulating glazing. Heat, in the form of long-wave radiation, flows from warm interior room surfaces and occupants to the cooler surface of the window. The heat cannot pass directly through the window because glass blocks long-wave radiation. Consequently, it is absorbed and readily conducted to the outer glass surface, where some of it, depending on the emissivity of the surface, is re-radiated. This process is repeated where there is a second or third layer of glass.

The higher the emissivity of the glass surface, the more heat is re-radiated (e = 0.84 in ordinary glass). Coating the glass with a low-emissivity layer or introducing a separate low-emissivity film between ordinary clear glazing can lower the emissivity of the glass and significantly reduce radiative heat loss. (See Figure 1.15.)

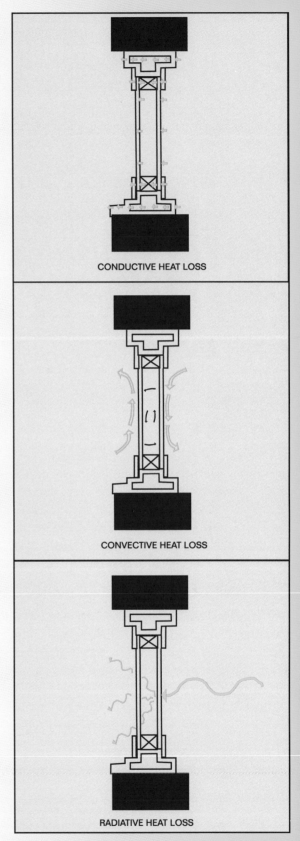

CONDUCTIVE HEAT LOSS

CONVECTIVE HEAT LOSS

RADIATIVE HEAT LOSS

FIGURE 1.14 Window heat transmission modes

9

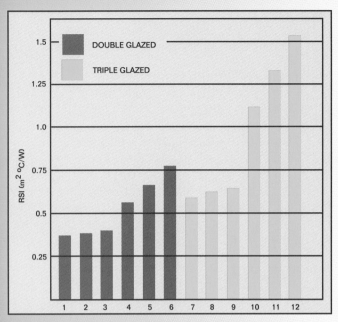

FIGURE 1.15 Effect of number of panes, coating and gas fill on centre-of-glass RSI value

1, 7.	Air-fill
2, 8.	Argon-fill
3, 9.	Krypton-fill
4, 10.	Low-e, air-ill
5, 11.	Low-e, argon-fill
6, 12.	Low-e, krypton-fill

Convection heat loss occurs at the inner and outer window surfaces and between the glass layers. Heat loss increases as the speed of the air circulating over the glass increases, lowering the insulating effect of the still air close to the surface. It is convection that causes increased heat loss on a windy day.

The speed of air circulation between the panes is also affected by the width of the air space in the window. For air-fill windows, a width of about 12.5 mm provides the lowest heat loss. With gases like krypton and argon, the best spacing is about 7 mm and 11 mm, respectively. Replacing the air with an inert, heavier-than-air gas or additional glass layers also reduces convection losses. (See Figure 1.15.)

Conduction heat loss occurs through the glass pane, the spacer and the window frame. Since the glass itself has virtually no insulating value, it is the surface air-film resistances that primarily lower the transmission of heat through the glazing. Insulating spacers between the glass panes can also reduce heat loss around the edges of the glass. Figure 1.16

shows how traditional metallic and newer insulating spacers affect heat transmission at the window's edge. Various types of insulating spacers have different performances.

Because this "edge effect" occurs over an approximately 65-mm-wide strip around the window, heat losses are highest in smaller windows. The benefit of insulating spacers is also more noticeable in high-performance glazings. For a small (500 mm x 500 mm), double-glazed, low-e, argon-filled window, the overall window RSI value would be 22 percent less than the centre-of-glass RSI value for metal spacers. However, it would be only 7 percent less for insulating spacers.

For a larger window (2,000 mm x 1,000 mm), these figures drop to 8 and 3 percent, respectively. Similar figures for a triple, low-e, argon-filled unit are higher—29 and 13 percent for the small window and 11 and 5 percent for the large window. Therefore, using one larger glazing unit rather than several smaller units, as in traditional divided-pane windows, helps to minimize overall heat loss. Muntin bars on the inside of the window reduce the edge heat losses associated with traditional divided panes. (A muntin bar is a central vertical piece of material between two panes of glass.)

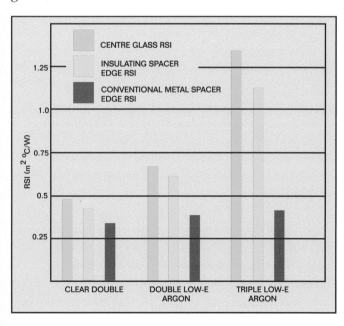

FIGURE 1.16 Effect of spacer type on edge-of-glass RSI values

Heat losses at the window frame vary with the frame's material and construction. Figure 1.17 shows a sample of different types of windows and their RSI values per unit area of frame. In addition, the smaller the frame, the lower the heat loss. Aluminum and fibreglass frames tend to be smaller than wood frames. Vinyl frames are usually larger.

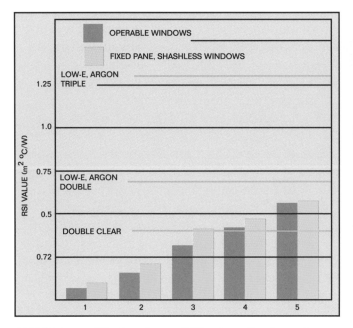

FIGURE 1.17 Window-frame RSI values (horizontal lines are centre-of-glass RSI values)

1. Aluminum
2. Thermal broken aluminum
3. Wood
4. Vinyl
5. Insulated fibreglass

Overall, aluminum and thermally broken aluminum windows tend to have the highest heat loss while insulated fibreglass frames have the lowest. However, the actual design and manufacturer determine the quality of the final product. Not only is the RSI value of the frame typically less than the glazing, but the frame does not transmit solar radiation This further reduces its performance relative to the glass. As window frames have lower RSI values than glazing, using fewer larger windows will reduce heat loss at the frame. Choosing windows on the basis of their ER value takes all this into account. (See Chapter 5 for more information on window frames.)

When comparing RSI values for windows, make sure the same values are being compared. Manufacturers often quote centre-of-glass RSI values (or R values) since these are always the highest values a window can have and are constant regardless of the window size. Comparing the centre-of-glass RSI value for one product against an overall RSI value for a window assembly can lead to the wrong choice.

Infiltration

Heat loss also results from the infiltration that occurs through the window and between the window and the wall. Fixed windows have less leakage than operable windows. In operable windows, it is the window type and seal design that determine leakage.

Window Energy Rating

The Canadian Energy Rating (ER) system is a simple method for comparing the energy efficiency of various windows. The ER system takes into account the effects of solar heat gain, heat transmission losses and air leakage. It is a measure of a window's average thermal performance, not an index of a window's superiority or inferiority in all situations. The ER value has units of W/m^2 and indicates the window's expected effect on the heating requirements of a house. It can vary widely depending on window type and can be either a positive or negative value. Figure 1.12 gives typical values for various types of windows.

A positive ER value means that the window contributes more heat to the house than it loses over a heating season. An ER value of zero indicates the window is energy neutral. In other words, it contributes as much solar heat to the house as it loses through heat transmission losses and infiltration. A zero-rated window is considerably better than a wall with an insulation level—or RSI value—of 3.5, which would have an ER value of -6.2.

Figure 1.12 also shows the difference in ER ratings between fixed and operable windows. This difference is partly due to increased infiltration, higher heat transmission and loss of solar gain through the operable sash. It is also the result of using different window sizes as the standard for fixed and operable windows. (See Table 1.1.) ER ratings for certified products are easy to compare because they are displayed on all new windows, but comparisons should only be made within a window category (i.e., fixed, casement, vertical slider, and so on).

Window Type	Width (mm)	Height (mm)
Vertical slider	920	1,550
Horizontal slider	1,550	920
Casement	600	1,220
Fixed	1,220	1,220
Sliding door	1,830	2,085

TABLE 1.1 Standard window sizes used for window energy rating

When using the ER system for comparing window performance, keep in mind the following limitations of the rating system.

• To make comparisons of products easy, the ER values displayed on windows have been calculated for standard window sizes. (See Table 1.1.) If a window is not of similar size to the standard, its annual performance may differ from the ER number. Moreover, different types of windows have different standard sizes. For example, the standard sliding window is almost twice as large as the standard casement. Therefore, comparisons between different types of windows should not be made. Generally, better performance would be expected from one large window than two smaller windows of equivalent area, especially if high-performance glazing is used.

• ER ratings are based on a typical dwelling in an average Canadian city, with glass equally distributed on all four sides. Average location and equal distribution are general assumptions and will not help with specific designs. Further, solar gains are counted as completely benefiting the heating of the house whenever the outdoor air temperature is below 13°C. In addition, as the area of glass increases, there is less usable solar heat gain and the ER values can overestimate the window's contribution to the home's energy needs.

For some passive solar applications, it is more helpful to establish a window's performance specific to its location and orientation because two windows with the same (averaged) ER rating can perform differently when facing south in different parts of the country.

To address these anomalies created by averaging, a Specific Energy Rating (ERS) method has been developed (CSA A440.2). It allows energy rating values to be calculated for specific locations, orientations and window size. (See Figure 1.18.) For further sophistication in selecting windows, house simulation programs such as HOT2000 can use data on U-value and SHGCs for ER-certified windows to accurately compare differences in window performance and obtain estimates of their energy savings.

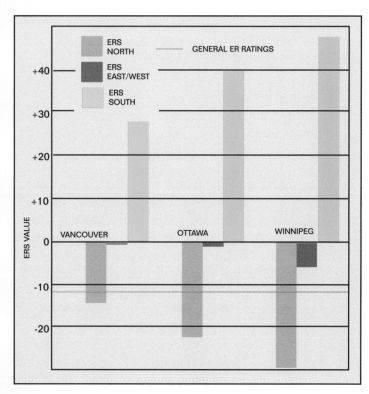

FIGURE 1.18 ERS values for typical, double low-e, argon-filled, wood-framed window

Winter Shading

During the heating season, it is best to avoid southern shading. In residential areas, the major cause of unwanted shading is usually adjacent buildings. (See Site Planning for Solar Access, page 48.) For individual, isolated houses, the main cause of unwanted shading is self-shading caused by window recesses and volume projections. For example, a garage sitting forward at the front of a dwelling is a common source of self-shading. (See Envelope Design, page 40.)

Window Recesses: As walls become thicker to accommodate more insulation, it is possible to locate windows towards the inside or the outside surface of the wall. From the standpoint of solar gain, it is better to install the window flush with the outside surface. This

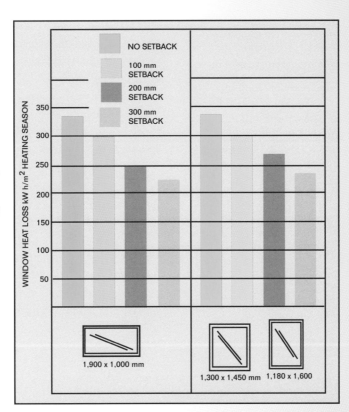

FIGURE 1.19 Effect of window recessing on winter heat gains through south-facing glazing (e.g., Ottawa)

prevents shading of the window by the top and side window reveals. (See also Window Mounting Options, page 31.) Further, the loss of solar heat gain is greatest with smaller windows. For units of similar area, windows with tall and narrow shapes have the greatest losses. (See Figure 1.19.)

Volume projections: In an extreme case, such as a south-facing window close to a large projection, self-shading can result in the loss of one half of the solar radiation falling on the window. Figure 1.20 illustrates self-shading by a volume projection to the south. The values shown are the percentage increases over a house without the projection. Incorrectly designed solar shading and landscaping can also reduce winter heat gains. (See Chapter 4.)

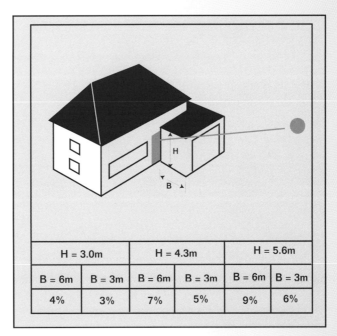

FIGURE 1.20 Increase in house heating consumption with self-shading

Summary

• Windows are the most important component in passive solar design.

• The angle dependency of solar transmission through windows makes south-facing glass an effective solar collector, allowing most gains in winter and rejecting most radiation in summer.

• A window's SHGC refers to the amount of solar energy it transmits. The bigger the SHGC, the better.

• Low-e coatings are suitable for passive solar applications because they reduce heat transmission losses with little loss of solar gain.

• The use of gases such as argon and krypton between windowpanes reduces heat losses by convection and improves a window's energy efficiency.

• Heat losses at the edge of a glass window are proportionately greater for smaller windows. Insulating spacers and window frames can reduce these losses.

• Using a few large windows gives better energy performance than more small ones.

• ER labelling is a quick and easy way to compare the performance of different windows. ERS and whole-house simulation provide a more sophisticated comparison.

The previous chapter focused on the critical role of windows as solar energy collectors. It discussed how energy is collected; the effect of various glazings; how dwellings lose heat; the use of energy ratings for comparing window performance; and how to avoid winter shading. Chapter 3 explains how to store and distribute solar energy throughout the house for maximum heating efficiency and comfort.

Room Heat Balance

Buildings constructed with heavy elements, such as concrete and masonry, have more stable internal temperatures than similar lightweight structures. The reason is that solar gain is stored in the building mass, preventing an abrupt rise of temperature, and is released as the space starts to cool, avoiding a sudden drop in temperature. Stable air temperatures mean improved comfort, and more stored solar heat means lower heating costs. To achieve stable and even temperatures, it is necessary to introduce heat storage and distribution.

When the sun's rays enter a room, they are partly reflected and partly absorbed by the room's surfaces. The absorbed radiation heats these surfaces which, in turn, raise the temperature of the surrounding air. Air circulation then transfers this heat to other spaces, where cooler surfaces reabsorb it.

Warmed surfaces also radiate heat by long-wave radiation to other room surfaces, including the windowpanes. But the windows, particularly those with low-e coatings, block long-wave radiation, trapping the heat in the room (the greenhouse effect) and raising the room temperature, sometimes above the comfort threshold.

Local overheating can occur when there is inadequate thermal mass or the air circulation fails to distribute the heat evenly. Temperatures above 25-26°C for prolonged periods will result in the occupants opening windows to adjust the room heat balance, which can have a negative effect on solar contribution and energy consumption.

Comfort Temperature Range

For heat storage to work, there must be temperature swings, the limits of which are dictated by comfort requirements. The temperature at which someone finds a room too warm is subjective and varies according to conditions such as the season, the humidity, the amount of clothing and the activity level. A temperature of 26°C might seem too warm if it is prolonged or accompanied by high humidity or activity levels. However, 26°C may be perfectly acceptable for short periods in the winter when the humidity is low. In a house, the occupants can also avoid or seek out sunny and warm rooms or adjust their clothing. In addition, the design of the house should make the opening of windows during winter unnecessary. A good design will limit the period during which temperatures are above 25°C to 4 percent of the heating season hours.

Typical Mass Effect: For a modestly glazed home, thermal mass has little effect on annual energy use, and overheating is not an issue. (See Figure 1.21, column 1.) However, a conventional wood-frame house will consume less energy than a heavy structure if the temperature is lowered in the evenings. (See Figure 1.21, column 2.) This difference is too small to be discernible in the illustration or make this a preferred strategy.

Buildings in which thermal mass has been incorporated behave differently. For example, in the passive solar home, an extra 150 kg of mass per square metre of floor area results in lower energy use and prevents the overheating associated with conventional wood-frame construction. (See Figure 1.21, columns 3 and 4.) This amount of mass is roughly the same as constructing three quarters of the interior partitions out of masonry. As a comparison of columns 3 and 4 in Figure 1.21 indicates, the use of a night setback schedule allows the thermal mass to be more effective.

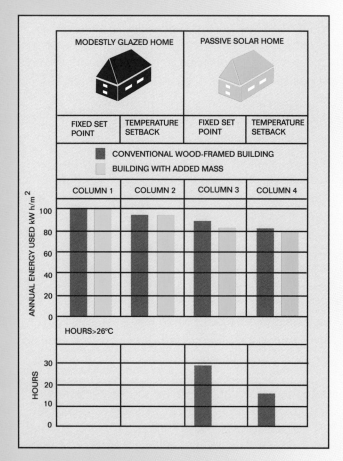

FIGURE 1.21 Interrelationship of thermal storage, heating consumption and temperature swing

Mass in Wood-frame Homes

Only when the ratio of south-facing glass to floor area exceeds 8 percent is it necessary to include more thermal mass in a conventional wood-frame house. To ensure overheating does not occur, make the best use of the mass by:

• arranging the windows to provide direct sunlight to as many rooms and surfaces as possible;

• locating less critical areas, such as circulation spaces, in direct sunlight, where higher temperatures will not affect comfort;

• providing good air circulation; and

• finishing lightweight elements in a room in light colours to distribute the reflected radiation evenly. This makes the best use of their limited thermal mass and helps distribute light more evenly throughout the space.

Adding Thermal Mass

Standard lightweight construction limits solar contribution because of its low heat capacity. Adding mass allows the use of more glazing for increased solar contribution without overheating. (See Figure 1.21.) Several materials, such as drywall, masonry, concrete and water, can be used to increase thermal mass. (See page 31 for guidance on the amount of mass to add.)

Figure 1.22 shows the specific heat capacity (per millimetre of material thickness per square metre of surface) for some common building materials. Using these values, it can be seen that 100 mm of masonry wall has 16 times the heat-storing capacity of 12 mm of gypsum board.

Not all layers of a mass element are equally useful for storing heat. Because heat flows are gradual,

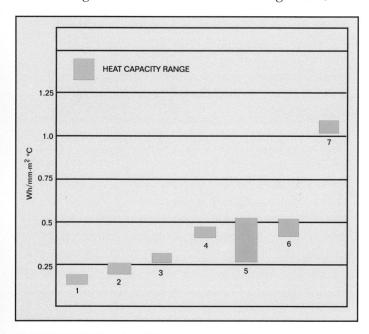

FIGURE 1.22 "Surface" heat capacity of some common materials

1. Plywood
2. Gypsum wallboard
3. Hardwoods
4. Clay masonry
5. Concrete masonry
6. Poured concrete
7. Water

the layers closest to the surface store more heat than the deeper layers. For passive solar applications, the charging of the mass during sunlight hours and the discharging during the night is very important. For this 24-hour cycle with modest temperature swings in room surface and air temperatures, the practical thickness of a mass element should be about 100 mm. Beyond that, very little is added to the storage capacity of the mass. A 50-mm layer is about two thirds as effective as a 100-mm thickness.

Just as important as the amount of mass added is its location relative to the windows. Unshaded, uncovered mass in direct sunlight is by far the most effective for heat storage. In fact, mass in direct sunlight is two times as effective as surfaces that receive indirect radiation in the same room, which are twice as effective as surfaces in a remote location.

Furniture, which typically has little mass, reduces the effectiveness of heat storage by shading the mass elements. Internal blinds have the same effect, and high window sills reduce the area of the floor receiving direct sunlight. The best location for heavy walls is as close as possible to the glazing, not at the back of deep rooms where they receive little direct sunlight.

When adding mass to floors, consider how the space will be used. Since a mass floor conducts heat quickly from surface to storage, it will do the same to warm feet, resulting in discomfort and the eventual covering of the floor. Try to locate mass floors where they are unlikely to be covered, or consider radiant floor heating for the house.

Carpets can reduce the heat-storage effectiveness of mass floors by up to 70 percent, and vinyl floor coverings by up to 50 percent. If the vinyl is dark, thin and well-secured, the effect can be limited to 5 to 10 percent. Circulation areas, such as the kitchen and breakfast rooms, are good locations for mass floors while sitting rooms are not.

Drywall: Thicker or multiple layers of drywall are a convenient and practical way to add mass. Using thicker or heavier fibre-reinforced drywall can help avoid an insulating air film that reduces heat flow into the second layer. (Fibre-reinforced drywall is 25 percent heavier than conventional drywall.)

Masonry and Concrete: Use brick, stone or concrete block for interior walls. Ceramic tile set on mortar or a layer of gypsum concrete can be added over a wood sub-floor. This will also improve fire integrity and reduce impact noise transmission.

Masonry is also a good choice for feature interior walls and fireplaces or for dividing walls between dwelling units. Other possibilities include adopting a slab or partial slab-on-grade design, or making use of the basement concrete floor by opening up the basement south wall with glazing.

Water: Water is exceptionally good for storing heat because it has twice the heat capacity of concrete. In addition, since convective currents readily distribute heat, more heat storage depth is available. Another benefit is that water, when stored in transparent containers, transmits light, although the view is distorted. However, the appearance, the possibility of leakage and water discolouration limit the use of such water-storage schemes.

Phase Change Materials: The amount of heat needed to melt a material is many times that required to raise its temperature by several degrees. By using a material with a melting point in the 15°C to 35°C range, large quantities of solar heat can be absorbed and stored in a relatively small volume. Building products, such as drywall, which use phase change materials are currently under development.

Remote Storage: Remote storage offers the potential of increasing a home's heat-storage capacity beyond what can be integrated into its walls and floors. A remote heat-storage system can be a bed of rock over which solar-heated room air is circulated or a water-storage tank charged by a heat pump operating between the solar-heated space and the water storage.

However, the energy required to move the solar heat to and from the storage medium, combined with losses from the storage, is often greater than the amount of solar energy used. This makes it hard to justify the cost of such a system. Generally, remote thermal storage is ineffective.

Mass Walls: Mass walls are exterior walls consisting of an outer glass layer, an air space and masonry or concrete. They are also referred to as thermal storage walls, Trombe walls or indirect-gains systems. Compared to a window, these walls allow more heat to be collected and slowly transferred to the room. In addition, because of the high air temperatures between the glass and the mass wall during sunlight hours, more effective use is made of the wall as a heat collector than as an interior wall.

The disadvantage of this system is the high heat loss that occurs because the wall is uninsulated to promote solar gains. Insulated and ventilated versions have been tried, but even with such improvements, these systems are not practical or cost effective for the Canadian climate.

Air Circulation

Air circulation distributes solar gain throughout the whole dwelling, distributing heat more evenly throughout the home. When solar gain exceeds total heat losses, air circulation allows those parts of the house not receiving direct radiation to store excess heat. Air circulation can be sustained either by natural convection or fans. To avoid consuming energy, use passive methods, such as natural convection, first.

Natural Convection: Natural air movement is driven by two factors: temperature difference and height. The taller the space, and the greater the temperature difference between the top and bottom of the space, the faster the air will circulate. Warmer, less dense air rises while cooler, denser air falls. Adding heat at a low level and extracting it at a high level will promote air circulation.

In addition, openings are needed for air circulation to occur, and the larger the openings, the better the

circulation. For air to flow between spaces, there needs to be a continuous air path or convective loop. (See Figure 1.23.) Parallel openings side by side in the convective loop will improve air circulation. Sequential openings through which the air must pass impose added resistance, with the smallest opening having the most limiting effect on the air flow. Increasing the size of the smaller opening to match the larger opening will increase the air flow.

COOL AIR FALLING
WARM AIR RISING

FIGURE 1.23 Natural convection in a dwelling

In general, to promote natural air circulation:

• keep floor plans compact;

• use large, open spaces;

• provide openings for air to flow between floors and between north and south zones (e.g., two-storey sunspaces and staircases arranged at opposite ends of the house);

• add mass at the top of the convective loop;

• locate glazing as low as practical in the convective loop;

• step the floors down toward the heat source to promote air circulation at the lower level; and

• add a sunspace where thermal comfort conditions can be relaxed—the greater the temperature differences between zones, the greater the air circulation. (See also Sunspaces, page 51.)

Forced Air Movement: Fans can help move the air. The furnace fan, for example, can operate in homes with forced-air heating. However, using fans to improve the effectiveness of solar energy can be counterproductive if it increases energy consumption. Running a furnace fan continuously during the heating season rather than letting it cycle with the demand for space heating can increase its energy consumption three-fold. (See Figure 2.5 and Mechanical Systems, page 42, for a detailed discussion on the use of fans.)

To minimize energy use, fans should have energy-efficient motors. Moreover, fans increase solar gain only if they operate when there is a useful temperature difference between south-facing spaces and the rest of the dwelling. The best way to minimize a fan's energy consumption is to use a cooling thermostat in the solar collecting space to turn on the fan automatically when its needed. The thermostat should be set 3-4°C above the normal heating set point.

Using supplementary fans to move the air between spaces is often an energy-saving way to circulate the air since there are no duct, furnace and diffuser friction losses. The use of slow-moving blade fans at the top of tall spaces, such as open staircases and two-storey sunspaces, is another way to redistribute heat and even out local temperature differences.

Summary

• Extra thermal mass results in lower energy consumption and prevents the overheating associated with wood-frame housing construction.

• Thermal mass allows the use of larger areas of south-facing glazing and provides improved solar gains and more stable indoor air temperatures.

• Unshaded, uncovered materials, such as concrete, masonry and extra-thick drywall, are most effective for storing heat when located in direct sunlight.

• Lowering the temperature of a space in the evening and during unoccupied periods increases the effectiveness of thermal mass.

• Remote heat storage systems are not effective thermally or in terms of cost.

• Good air circulation uses mass elements throughout the house and evens out temperature differences between the rooms.

• To promote good air circulation, houses should be compact and open with large openings between the floors.

• A furnace can provide enough air circulation to circulate heat effectively. If the fan is used to distribute solar gains, operate it only when the temperature in sunlit rooms is 3-4°C higher than in cooler rooms. The fan should have a high-efficiency motor.

4. Shading and Summer Comfort

The previous chapter introduced the concept of thermal mass and explained how it stores heat and helps prevent overheating. It also described how materials, such as drywall, masonry and concrete, can augment the effect of thermal mass, and how air circulation systems distribute heat evenly throughout a house.

One of the main objectives of passive solar design is to ensure that the home remains comfortable throughout the summer and requires little or no air conditioning. This chapter explains the importance of shading for preventing solar gains, and how to ensure good ventilation for cooling.

Achieving occupant comfort is also dealt with in greater technical detail in Chapter 8. (Appendix 2 provides instructions on how to use the *Comfort Design Checker* software.)

The best way to reduce solar gains is to shade the windows from the outside. The shading can be fixed, removable or adjustable. Adjustable and removable shading are the most effective because they provide the exact amount of sunlight or shade required. Fixed shading is normally of a size that produces a balance between losing heat and daylight in the winter and excluding heat in the summer.

Shading that is effective and beneficial in August and September will reduce solar gain in March and April, when it would be welcome. In addition, shading excludes some diffuse radiation all year. Therefore, it is important that shading be designed to match the requirements of location and orientation. It should also strike a balance between admitting and excluding sunlight throughout the year.

Overhangs and Awnings

On south-facing windows, horizontal overhangs provide effective shading and limit heat gains in the spring, summer and fall. They are less effective on east- or west-facing windows because of the low angle of the sun, unless the projections are very wide, such as a carport or porch.

Solid overhangs give the best shading because they block both direct and diffuse radiation. Slatted overhangs partially reflect the sun's rays. Translucent overhangs allow radiation to pass through according to their transmission characteristics. (See Table 1.2.)

Type of Window Treatment	Shade Reflectance (c)
INTERIOR VENETIAN BLINDS (a)	
Light	35%
VERTICAL BLINDS	
Light closed	60%
ROLLER BLINDS	
Dark opaque	20%
White opaque	60%
EXTERIOR FABRIC SHADES (b)	**60 - 88%**
EXTERIOR LOUVRED SUNSCREENS (a)	
Light	88%
Dark	85%
DRAPERIES AND PLEATED BLINDS (b)	
Light open weave	28%
Light close weave	40%
Reflective lined	60%

TABLE 1.2 Solar shading characteristics of some common window treatments

Notes:
(a) Value when excluding all direct sunlight
(b) Values vary widely
(c) Tabulated values represent the amount of solar heat reflected by the shade

The best practical compromise for a south-facing overhang is to ensure that the window is completely unshaded at the winter solstice (December 21 or 22) and between fully and half-shaded at noon on the summer solstice (June 21 or 22). Figure 1.24 illustrates this point graphically. (See Appendix I for tables of solar altitude at noon.)

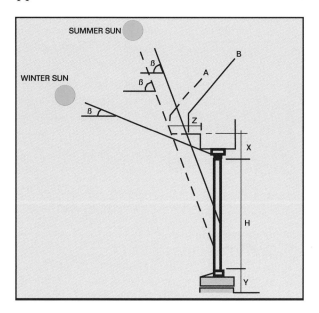

FIGURE 1.24 Overhang sizing

Roofline A provides shading over the entire window.
Roofline B provides shading over half the window

X	=	Eave-to-glass distance
H	=	Window height
Y	=	Window sill height
Z	=	Overhang projection
ß	=	Solar altitude at noon

In summer, a south-facing window will remain shaded all day if it is shaded at noon and if the overhang extends past the edges of the window. (See Figure 1.25.) Locating the overhang above the window will only ensure that the top portion of the window does not stay shaded all year.

For upper-storey windows, the eave-to-glass distance is 320 mm to 370 mm. This is usually the sum of the depth of the window frame,

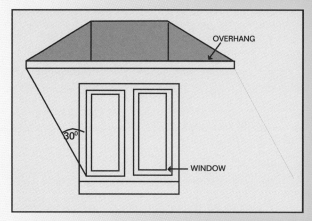

FIGURE 1.25 Overhang side projection

To ensure that the window is fully shaded, the overhang should extend beyond the window as shown

window lintel and top plates. For lower floors, overhangs can be located and shaped to create the best shading.

For south-facing glazing, the maximum overhang projection that will leave the glass unshaded in winter for two eave-to-glass distances is shown in Figure 1.26 for a range of Canadian latitudes. Increasing the distance and extending the overhang provides more complete summer shading without losing heat gains in winter.

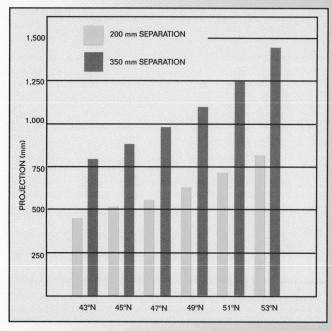

FIGURE 1.26 Maximum overhang projection

Projection (metres) required to avoid winter shading on south-facing windows

Figure 1.27 gives the sizes of the projections needed for full and half shading in Ottawa (45°N) for three different windows with a 350-mm eave-to-glass distance. Higher latitudes and off-south orientations call for larger projections to give full window shading.

Louvred Overhangs: Open louvred overhangs are an option for extra-deep shades. These might be required on tall windows or for off-south orientations where add-on shades are necessary. Louvred overhangs are lighter than the solid variety, do not collect snow or water, are less affected by wind and allow more light to enter the window.

In the summer, larger louvred overhangs do not trap heat that could eventually enter the dwelling through open windows. Unlike solid overhangs, they transmit diffuse solar radiation, which is a benefit in winter but a drawback in summer. Adding a shade cloth in summer or training a deciduous vine over the overhang will improve the shading.

Angling the louvres towards the sun permits some direct radiation to enter during the winter. For a south-facing window, the best slat angle for minimum winter shading is equal to the solar altitude at noon in midwinter. For maximum

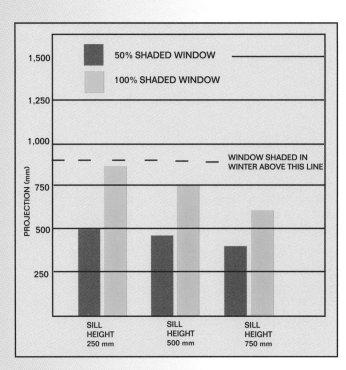

FIGURE 1.27 Overhang projection to provide full and half shading in summer for Ottawa (45°N, 350-mm separation)

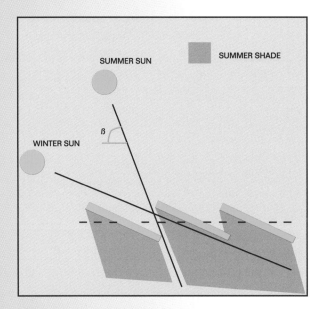

FIGURE 1.28 Slot geometry for slat-type overhangs (ß = solar altitude at noon on June 21)

summer shading, arrange the slats to block all direct sunlight at noon on June 21. (See Figure 1.28.)

Because louvres pass some diffuse and some direct radiation, larger projections can be used. Using a dark colour for the slats will increase the shading effectiveness of the overhang. The same applies to solid overhangs but with an anticipated greater reduction of winter solar gains, which increases as the length of the overhang increases.

Awnings: The awning is another form of overhanging shade. Awnings featuring side wings and a drop below the window head provide complete shading with smaller projections and without the need to extend the shade past the window edges. The sun's rays will be partially reflected, partially absorbed and partially transmitted. These awnings are particularly useful for east- and west-facing windows.

To assess the performance of awnings, it is important to understand their solar optical properties. Table 1.2 provides typical values, but specific data for the type of material being considered should be used. Highly reflective, open-weave materials are preferred because they limit heat build-up under the awning.

One advantage of an awning is that it is easily adjusted. This allows the shades to be raised on overcast summer days for better daylighting. In winter, awnings can be removed to avoid the reduction of solar gain.

Window Treatments and Shades

There are a variety of add-on window treatments, including blinds, shutters, screens and drapes. Some treatments, such as window tinting and films, are integral parts of the glazing system. However, tints and films are not suitable for passive solar applications because they cause a reduction of solar gains during the heating season. By contrast, internal shades often have an adjustment that lets the occupant control summer heat gains and avoid the reduction of heat gains during the winter.

Louvres: Louvred sunshades can be fixed or adjustable. Fixed, exterior louvred sunshades provide shade all year round and must be opened or removed during winter. Smaller-size louvres have better transparency. Mini-louvres maintain the view without the obstruction caused by large louvres. Inside louvred blinds can be either horizontal or vertical, and both types are adjustable. In light colours, they absorb less radiation and conduct less heat.

Shutters: Shutters are hinged devices, normally solid or with openings, that allow air to circulate and prevent heat build-up between the shutter and the window. Casement-type shutters that open can be installed on the inside or outside of the house. When insulated, shutters can reduce a window's heat transmission.

Fabrics: There are many fabrics suitable for use both inside and outside the house. Table 1.2 on page 23 gives the effective shading factors for a range of common window treatments. To find the Solar Heat Gain Coefficient (SHGC) for the blind and window combination, subtract the tabulated value from 1, then multiply by the window's SHGC value. (The tabulated values were compiled for each shade with clear double glazing.)

When curtains or blinds are in their parked condition, windows should be completely unshaded. In addition, the curtain rails should extend beyond the edge of the window. Vertical blinds should be installed so that, when open, they do not obstruct any portion of the window.

Common Name	5-yr. Growth (m) (a)	Typical Mature Height (m)	Spread	Shape (b)	% Shade (c)
Mountain Ash	6.0	6–12	6–12	Round	40–50
Larch	n.a.	12–18	n.a.	Col	20–40
Manitoba Maple	5.0	12–18	12–18	Round	87
Poplar	10	15–25	4.5–5.5	Col	40
Green Ash	5.0	15–18	6–9	Col	38–66
Little Leaf Linden	3.5	15–20	7.5–10.5	Con	65
Paper Birch	4.0	25–30	12–15	Round	20–60
American Elm	3.5	15–18	9–12	Col	28–42
Manchurian Elm	3.5	12–15	12–15	Round	62
Weeping Birch	2.5	10–12	10	Weep	54–66

TABLE 1.3 Shade characteristics for some popular shade trees bare of leaf

Notes:
Not all trees may be hardy in all climatic zones

(a) Approximate growth rate for newly planted 2.5–3-m tree
(b) Col = Columnar; Con = Conical; Weep = Weeping
(c) Actual shading can be reduced by pruning

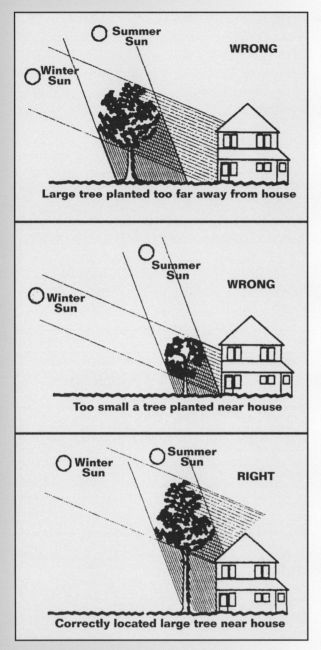

FIGURE 1.29 Shadow patterns from south-planted trees

Detached Shading

Detached shading usually means trees or shrubs. In addition to providing shade, trees reduce a home's cooling needs by cooling the air through leaf evaporation and by shading hard surfaces.

For passive solar heating, trees that lose their leaves in the fall are the best because they minimize the reduction of heat gain during winter. Other important considerations are the tree's location, its initial size, growth rate and ultimate size, as well as its sunlight transmission characteristics when in-leaf and bare. All these factors must be considered if trees are not to become a liability, causing shading that prevents heat gain when it is needed.

As a general rule, trees should not be located directly south of the house. Even a deciduous tree, bare of leaf, can cast enough shadow to impair the performance of south-facing glazing. (See Table 1.3.) In winter, large deciduous trees can block more than 50 percent of the sun's rays. If there must be a tree to the south, it should be a single-trunked, tall-growing variety close to the house, and the lower branches should be removed as the tree grows. Figure 1.29 shows the shadow patterns cast by south-planted trees.

The best location for shade trees is to the east and west. Avoid locating trees so far south along the east and west sides of the site that they block the sunlight falling on the south-facing windows.

During the winter, most heat is collected between 9:00 a.m. and 3:00 p.m. Therefore, a 30° angle on either side of the north-south axis should be kept clear in front of all south-facing windows (See Figure 1.30.) If trees must be planted within this space, use Figure 1.30 and Table 1.4 to determine the required distance for a particular direction and species.

Ventilation

Properly oriented glazing and well-designed shading should ensure low solar gains in summer. Ventilation will also remove unwanted heat generated by lighting and household appliances, as well as the natural heat given off by the occupants during normal activities. Natural ventilation, which does this without consuming energy, is better than a mechanical ventilation system. The latter should be used only as a supplement to natural ventilation on hot, windless days.

Natural Ventilation: In summer, natural ventilation makes a home more comfortable and reduces or eliminates the need for air conditioning. Operable windows equal to between 6 and 8 percent of the floor area should provide sufficient natural cooling, except on hot, humid, windless days.

The following are ways to enhance natural ventilation.

• Ensure cross-ventilation by locating operable windows on opposite walls in the direction of the prevailing summer winds.

• Locate operable windows with as much vertical separation as possible by using clerestory windows, cupolas or vents in the roof.

• Adopt open-plan designs.

Mechanical Ventilation: In summer, it is better to ventilate the whole house with a supplementary fan than to use the furnace fan with modified duct work that draws in outside air. The supplementary fan should change the inside air about 10 times an hour. It should be located at the highest point in the house, where it can vent the warmest air and allow cooler outside air to be drawn in through open windows. Ducts should be as short as possible to minimize the fan's energy consumption.

The fan opening in the wall should be sealed and insulated to avoid heat losses in winter. Whole-house fans should be controlled by a cooling action thermostat or, better still, by an indoor-outdoor thermostat that keeps the fan from operating if the outdoor temperature equals or exceeds the indoor temperature.

Ceiling Fans: By generating air movement of between 0.50 and 0.75 m/s, ceiling fans can provide a level of comfort equal to 2°C cooler in still air. (Whole-house ventilation fans cannot create such speeds.) The fans should be located close to and directly above places such as a beds or sitting areas.

Placing fans in tall spaces, such as a double-height sunspace or stairwell, will not cool the house sufficiently since they will only push the warmer upper air to the floor rather than exhaust it.

Thermal Mass: Thermal mass delays a dwelling's response to rising temperatures, keeping it cool except during prolonged hot spells. If cooler night air flows over heavy elements, such as concrete or masonry, it will help remove heat that has been stored there during the day and lower the temperature for the next day.

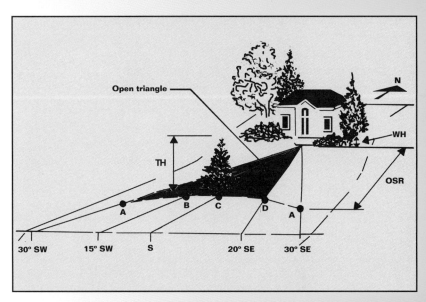

FIGURE 1.30 Trees planted on the south side of a dwelling

OSR = (TH-WH) x CF
Key:
OSR = Open space required
TH = Tree height at maturity
WH = Window height (distance from bottom of window to ground)
CF = Clearance factor (to be worked out using Table 1.4)

Northern Latitude	Corresponding Cities	A	B	C	D
44°	Toronto and Halifax	3.2	2.6	2.4	2.8
46°	Fredricton, Québec, Montréal and Ottawa	3.6	2.9	2.6	3.1
48°	St. John's	4.1	3.2	3.0	3.5
50°	Winnipeg and Vancouver	4.8	3.6	3.4	4.0
53°	Edmonton	6.1	4.5	3.7	5.0

TABLE 1.4 Clearance factors

Summary

- Shading controls heat gains in summer.

- The most effective shading is adjustable and installed outside the window.

- East- and west-facing windows are the hardest to shade. Louvred overhangs and awnings provide the most effective shading.

- Fixed overhangs should leave the windows completely unshaded at the winter solstice and between fully and half shaded at noon on the summer solstice.

- Exterior awnings and shutters offer better summer shading than fixed overhangs, without losing winter heat gains.

- Interior blinds and drapes, while not as effective as outside devices, can be easily adjusted and provide useful shading.

- Do not plant trees directly south of the building. Trees within 45° of the southeast and southwest corners of the building provide useful shade for east- and west-facing windows during the summer and prevent shading during the winter.

- Natural ventilation makes a home comfortable in summer and reduces the need for air conditioning. The ratio of operable window area to floor area should be 6 to 8 percent. Locate the windows to promote both stack and cross-ventilation.

- Use separate whole-house fans to supplement natural ventilation.

- Ceiling fans help maintain comfort during hot periods.

Chapter 4 explained how to prevent solar energy from making a house too hot. It discussed shading the windows with overhangs, awnings, louvres and shutters, as well as planting trees and ensuring proper ventilation. Windows are also important for creating the right daylighting and for their effect on comfort, condensation resistance and sound transmission. These and other window and building envelope issues are the focus of Chapter 5.

Basic Window Types

Windows come in a variety of types, and each type has its advantages and disadvantages, as described below.

Fixed or picture windows: These windows have the lowest possible air leakage and are often coupled with awnings or casements that provide ventilation. Fixed windowpanes are set directly into the window frame while operable windows are set in a sash. This avoids unnecessary heat losses through the window frame by reducing the number of frame members through which heat loss can occur. It also provides more glass area and is less expensive.

Casement Windows: When closed, casement windows have low air leakage because the opening windowpane is drawn tightly against a compression bulb or fin-type air seal. Casement windows also provide the entire open area for ventilation. For summer cooling, the opening should swing into the prevailing wind to provide more ventilation.

Awning and Hopper Windows: These windows are similar to casements but they hinge horizontally. The ventilation opening depends on the height of the window, which is usually more than 300 mm but is limited by the practical length of the window support hardware. For large windows, the effective ventilation opening can be significantly smaller than the operable sash size. Awning windows can ventilate the house even when it is raining.

Vertical Sliders: Vertical sliders are not as airtight as casement and awning windows since they rely on a sliding seal. Nor are the seals likely to have the same longevity because the window sash moves along them. Consequently, condensation can be a problem near the centre rail. Vertical sliders can be double-hung, with both the top and bottom halves of the window operable, or single-hung, with only the lower sash operable.

The double-hung type offers better ventilation than casement and awning windows because it is more effective at removing warmer ceiling air. It also has more air leakage since the length of the crack is almost doubled. In addition, the ventilation opening is limited to slightly less than half the overall window size.

Horizontal Sliders: These units are similar to double-hung windows. They are generally leaky, but some high-quality products have good performance. Energy ratings are comparable to casements and could be better as a result of thinner sash members.

Glass Block: Like other fixed windows, those constructed from glass blocks have low air leakage. Because of their ruggedness, security and durability, they provide good daylighting, with some physical, visual and acoustic privacy. However, they are a poor choice for reducing energy consumption as they have a low SHGC and half the RSI value of a double-glazed, low-e window.

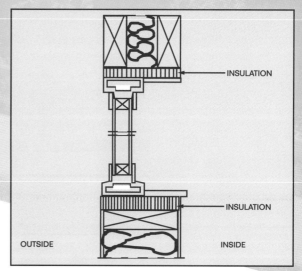

FIGURE 1.31 Window rough opening insulation detail

Insulating between the window frame and the rough opening prevents thermal bridging

Wall Framing

Windows require additional framing. As a result, thermal bridging through the building envelope will increase around windows. The following are a few ways to minimize this effect:

• locate and size the windows to coincide with normal stud spacing;

• insulate the inside or outside surface of the studs for the whole house;

• insulate the window reveals, head and below the sill (see Figure 1.31); and

• use fewer larger windows instead of several smaller ones.

Window Mounting Options

Locating windows towards the inside wall surface has the following advantages:

• lower heat loss because of higher outdoor film resistance due to slower air movement over the sheltered glass surface;

• reduced thermal bridging through the sill and framing around the window opening; and

• reduced risk of condensation because the air velocity over the inside glass layer is higher.

However, this method of mounting requires a wide exterior sill and can create waterproofing problems. (See Figure 1.32.) On the other hand, locating the window towards the outer face of the wall has other benefits, including:

• greater solar gains;

• increased inside film resistance;

• simplified window reveal and sill detailing; and

• the creation of a useful ledge.

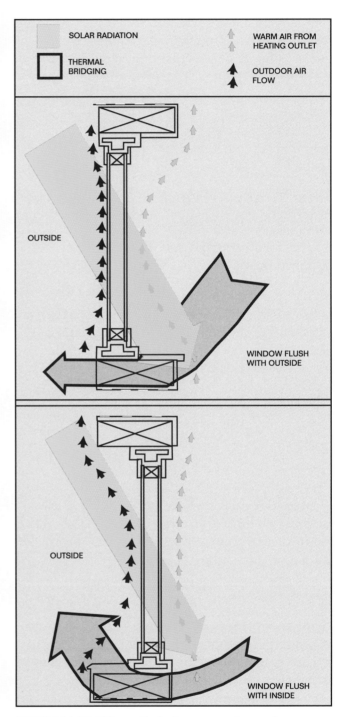

FIGURE 1.32 Effect of window mounting on heat gains and losses

As the window's RSI value increases, the loss of heat due to lower outdoor air film resistance is proportionately less significant, and condensation risk due to lower indoor air velocity at the glass surface diminishes. The combined effect of these two factors suggests a window location toward the outer face of the wall.

Whether the window is located towards the inner or outer wall surface, insulation between the window and the rough frame opening will reduce thermal bridging. (See Figure 1.31.) Thicker shims will be required at the window support points. Windows set towards the outside face of the wall will benefit the most as this placement reduces the loss of solar heat absorbed on the window sill and reveals. In practice, windows are usually located at some mid-distance dictated by the manufacturer's design.

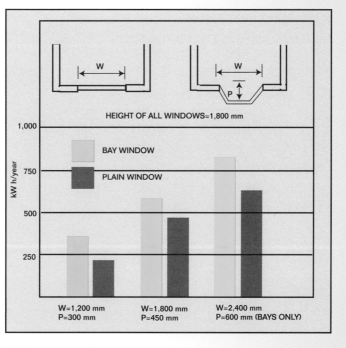

FIGURE 1.33 Comparison of bay and plain window heating season net heat balance (windows face due south)

Windows as Design Elements

Bay Windows: Bay windows increase the amount of glass without proportionately increasing the amount of solar gain because the exterior wall opening is not increased. In fact, bay windows have worse energy performance than ordinary windows in a similar-sized opening. (See Figure 1.33.) Typically, bay windows are installed for aesthetic reasons and for the extra view they provide.

Solar Bays: Solar bays are a specific type of bay window. Their application is limited to east and west orientations, with only the south-facing section of the bay being glazed. Used on the side walls of houses that are overshadowed by a neighbouring property, solar bays provide a better view than normal windows because they project out from the wall. They also provide visual privacy and solar collection. Their solar collection is significantly less than an unobstructed south window but more than an obstructed east- or west-facing window. The main drawback is that a bay projecting from the house increases the overall envelope heat loss. Having a triangular rather than a rectangular bay will minimize this loss.

Garden Windows: Garden windows are small bay windows with outdoor sills and no projecting floor area. They are usually glazed on three vertical sides and sometimes on top. Garden windows are even less energy-efficient than bay windows.

Dormers: Dormers are projecting vertical windows in the sloping roof a house. They provide a view, daylighting and additional floor area for attics. However, the extra roofing and walls around the window increase overall heat losses. Depending on the framing details and the level of insulation, these losses may be greater than curb losses associated with skylights.

While windows are normally positioned to provide a view, some can be added solely for admitting daylight or solar gains. The most common of these are clerestory windows, cupolas and skylights.

Clerestory Windows: Clerestory windows are located in the upper part of the exterior wall of the house. They are generally fixed because of the difficulty of providing a means of operation. When they face south, they provide solar gains to north-facing rooms. If they can be opened, their enhanced stack effect increases natural ventilation.

Cupolas: Cupolas are small, rounded roof domes, glazed all around, that serve the same purpose as clerestory windows. Compared to the clerestory window, their 360° glazing provides good daylighting but reduced thermal performance. This is the result of heat loss and lack of solar gains through their northerly glazing.

Skylights: Skylights can be installed on horizontal or inclined roofs. They can also cause overheating because they collect most solar heat in the warmer months of the year. (See Figure 1.3.) Another problem with skylights is that they lose heat through roof curbs and the walls of the light-well constructed in an unheated attic. These losses are exacerbated because warm air rises and temperatures are higher in the attic than in the rest of the dwelling. For the lowest heat losses, skylights should be installed on insulated curbs and not over attics requiring large light-wells. It is best to avoid skylights for passive solar heating, but they do admit daylight for balancing room light levels and illuminating deep open spaces.

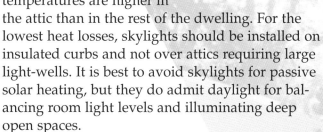

Corner Windows: Avoid windows that wrap around a corner or abut both sides of it. Solar radiation entering on one side can pass directly out the other.

Window Frames

Wood, aluminum, polyvinyl chloride (PVC), fibreglass and steel are all used to construct window frames and sashes. These materials are most commonly used alone but can be used in combination to take advantage of their various desirable properties.

Wood: Wood is a relatively good insulator. Until the advent of newer, high-performance windows, it was a better insulator than the glazing. However, the absorption of moisture can cause wood to warp and twist, resulting in windows that are hard to operate and the possibility of greater air infiltration. In addition, the absorption of moisture promotes rot. To prevent these problems, wood windows require painting or staining initially and every few years.

Clad Wood Window: To reduce maintenance, PVC or aluminum cladding is added to the outside of the wood frames. This cladding must be watertight and must not retain any water that leaks between it and the wood frame because trapped moisture promotes rot. Clad wood windows require that the caulked joints be checked and maintained regularly. To prevent increased heat loss, the aluminum cladding must not come into contact with the glass surface.

Aluminum: These windows are made of hollow extruded sections of aluminum. Because aluminum conducts heat, the inner and outer window sections must be separated by a low-conducting thermal break. Even with thermal breaking, it is difficult to manufacture low-heat-loss frames. The benefits of aluminum are strength, durability and low maintenance.

Vinyl: Vinyl, or PVC, windows are constructed somewhat like aluminum windows, but the section tends to contain smaller air spaces, and the frames are welded rather than mechanically fixed. Vinyl is not as good a conductor of heat as aluminum and has heat loss comparable to wood windows.

However, large vinyl windows often need steel reinforcement to increase their rigidity, which increases their ability to conduct heat. Further, with vinyl windows, expansion and contraction joint and sealant design is critical to performance. To minimize their ability to conduct heat, these windows are normally manufactured in light colours to absorb less radiation. Vinyl windows do not require regular maintenance.

Fibreglass: Fibreglass windows, which are relatively new, consist of hollow sections mechanically fastened together. They can be foam-filled for improved energy efficiency. Fibreglass offers the same benefits as vinyl, with potentially more strength and rigidity and less thermal expansion.

As with all materials, the thinner the section, the better the thermal performance. Good vinyl and fibreglass frames should perform slightly better than wood frames. But poorly designed vinyl and fibreglass frames will perform well below wood.

When evaluating frames, compare the window energy ratings and condensation resistances. This is particularly important with aluminum frames as it is hard to judge whether a frame is made with an effective thermal break.

Condensation

Condensation can form on a window's interior surface if any part of the window is cold enough. Indoor humidity, outside temperature, incident solar radiation and air movement over the window all affect condensation. Air entering through the window can also create cold spots and increase the likelihood of condensation.

Occasional and minimal condensation is not a problem. But persistent and heavy condensation speeds up the deterioration of surface finishes and can lead to mould growth, rot and premature failure of the glazing seal. Higher-performance windows reduce centre-of-glass condensation problems as long as the indoor humidity is not excessive. The use of insulating spacers and less conductive frames can reduce edge-of-glass and frame condensation.

The frame performance illustrated in Figure 1.34 assumes that there are no thermal bridges in the frame. If there are thermal bridges, localized condensation at humidities lower than those shown can be expected. If the window is not labelled, contact the supplier to find out the condensation resistance of the product.

Maintaining air flow over the inside of the window minimizes condensation build-up by raising the window's surface temperature slightly and re-evaporating any condensation. In the past, it

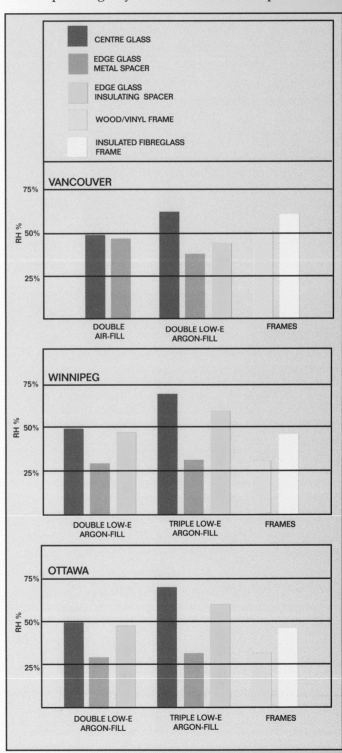

FIGURE 1.34 Indoor humidity at which condensation will form (winter design conditions)

was common practice to locate an air supply grille under the window and set the window flush with the inside wall. Higher-performance windows make this unnecessary today.

Even with the above precautions or the use of high-performance windows, condensation can form once the drapes are drawn over the window. Therefore, it is best to choose windows that satisfy the conditions shown in Figure 1.34, with a margin of safety.

With very tightly constructed houses, the indoor humidity can become high enough to create condensation on the windows. A properly designed and sized mechanical ventilation system, as required by codes, should be able to control excess humidity. A two-speed heat-recovery ventilation system operated on high speed under the control of a humidistat is an energy efficient way to control intermittent humidity problems.

Thermal Comfort

Thermal comfort is the product of air temperature, radiant temperature, humidity, air velocity, the amount of clothing worn and activity level. Windows directly affect the first four of these factors.

At night and during overcast winter days, cold window surfaces lower the temperature in a room and create cold-air drafts. Air leaking through the window creates additional cold drafts and further reduces humidity levels. To be comfortable under these circumstances, occupants usually have to raise the thermostat to a higher setting.

With the winter sun shining, the surface temperature of the window rises a little as solar radiation heats the room surfaces and increases the room's temperature. Under these circumstances, occupants feel naturally comfortable. In summer, when cooler temperatures are needed, sunlight entering the room raises the air temperature and creates discomfort. Therefore, ventilation and shading are required to maintain the house at a comfortable temperature.

The following are a few practical ways to improve comfort.

• **Window RSI Values.** The higher the RSI value of the window, the higher its surface temperature and the warmer the room. For example, at an outside temperature of -27°C, a conventional double-glazed window has a surface temperature 18°C cooler than the inside temperature. With a triple-glazed, low-e, argon-filled window, the difference is only 5°C. Windows with higher RSI (i.e., insulation) values also support higher humidity levels and reduce drafts.

• **Window Area.** Reduce the window area to lower the overall effect of the cold surface. This is another reason for minimizing all but south-facing glazing.

• **Window Size.** Redistribute or eliminate tall windows. They create cold-air drafts that move towards and across the floor and make sitting near windows uncomfortable.

• **Window Location.** Locate windows as far from seating areas as practical to minimize the effects of cold drafts. Cold air warms by 2-3°C per metre travelled.

• **Window Sills.** Provide a window sill that will interrupt the flow of cold air down the wall and limit its travel along the floor into the room.

• **Heating Outlets.** Locate grilles or radiators under the window to overcome cold drafts and raise the surface temperature of the glass. (This will result in a marginal increase in heat loss through the window.) Radiators with controlled output that is proportionate to heat loss provide continuous protection from drafts. Systems that operate in an on-off mode, like most furnaces, are effective only when the thermostat calls for heat. If furnaces are oversized, protection from drafts could be lost even during the coldest weather.

• **Draperies**. Heavy drapes with heat reflecting linings can help eliminate cold drafts on winter nights. (There is an increased risk of condensation with this measure.)

• **Shades.** Window shades, particularly on the exterior of the house, improve summer comfort by reducing the surface temperatures of the window and the room and by blocking direct sunlight.

Daylighting

Windows not only provide useful heating, they can reduce your dependence on electric lighting and lower energy costs. Passive solar design calls for south-facing windows, but it is important not to neglect daylighting in other parts of the dwelling.

When planning for good daylighting, consider the illumination provided by the sky rather than direct sunlight, which is often undesirable. Outside illuminance is constantly changing. Therefore, it is usual to define the level of day-lighting provided in the space as a percentage of the outside illuminance. This is known as the "Daylight Factor." Daylight and the Daylight Factor can vary in different parts of the room.

Table 1.5 gives the recommended values for aver-age and minimum Daylight Factor. A 2 percent Daylight Factor provides about 160 lx at noon on an overcast day in December and 300 lx on a partly cloudy day. By the spring equinox (about March 21), these values will have risen to 260 lx and 1,000 lx, respectively.

Room	Daylight Factor %	
	Average	Minimum
Living	1.50	0.50
Bedrooms	1.00	0.30
Kitchens	2.00	0.60
Home/Office/Hobby	2.00 (on work surface)	

TABLE 1.5 Recommended values of Daylight Factor

For general illumination, 100 lx is sufficient, and between 300 and 750 lx is desirable for kitchens and office or hobby areas. A 2 percent Daylight Factor can be achieved with a window area equal to 10 percent of the floor area. This is the minimum glass area for kitchens and living rooms required by the National Building Code. (The minimum for bedrooms is 5 percent.)

Higher levels, particularly in areas like kitchens and workrooms, are desirable to avoid the frequent use of electric lights. They may also be needed for healthy plant growth. However, many species of plants will do well in lower levels of light. (See Table 2.1 for examples.)

Good daylighting is not simply a function of the quantity of light. In fact, some techniques that increase the quantity of daylight can actually decrease its quality. The two main quality issues are glare and light distribution. Glare can be either disabling or discomforting. It is disabling when it interferes with the ability to see. It is discomforting when there is excessive contrast between light and dark surfaces in a room. Glare does not necessarily increase with increasing window size.

The following considerations should be taken into account when attempting to achieve the best level of daylighting.

• **Glass Type:** Glazing that allows the highest transmission of the visible portion of the solar spectrum provides the highest daylight levels. High SHGC implies high light transmittance. This makes the need for daylighting compatible with the need for passive solar heating.

• **Window Position:** The higher the window, the greater the Daylight Factor and the deeper the penetration of daylight into the space. Extending the window to the floor does little to increase day-light levels. Clerestory windows that allow deep penetration of daylight while avoiding normal viewing angles are a good daylighting strategy.

Spreading the windows out along a wall (Figure 1.35, Scheme B) results in a more even illumination than a single, centrally located window (Figure 1.35, Scheme A). Placing windows on two or more adjacent walls (Figure 1.35, Scheme C) improves the quality of daylighting by increasing the uniformity of the lighting and reducing shadows. Locating a window close to an end wall has an effect that is similar to but smaller than reflecting daylight off the wall. For maximum effect, the wall should be a light colour.

In deep rooms, adding a skylight or clerestory glazing towards the centre of the room (Figure 1.35, Scheme D) can improve daylight penetration and uniformity. Clerestory glazing has better thermal performance than skylights, and skylights are better than side windows when the windows are shaded by an adjacent dwelling. For maximum daylighting, windows should have unobstructed views of the sky.

• **Room Finishes:** For maximum daylight levels, uniformity and the least glare, room surfaces should have matte finishes. Shiny finishes create reflections that result in glare.

• **Window Shades:** Use sheers or adjustable blinds to reduce window brightness or block out bright patches of sky light. Some loss of solar energy is inevitable, but this can be minimized with judicial use of shades.

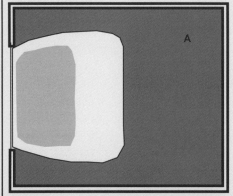
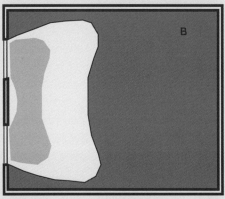
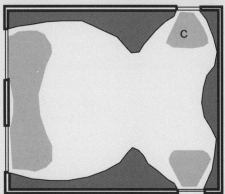
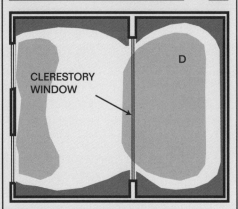

CLERESTORY WINDOW

FIGURE 1.35 Daylight variation for different fenestration designs

• **Space Planning:** For a given window arrangement, daylight levels will be higher and more uniform in an open-plan space than a highly partitioned one.

Sound Transmission

Windows are the weak link in the sound insulating performance of a building envelope. For most dwellings, noise transmission through the envelope is not a major issue. It becomes a problem when dwellings are located close to airports or busy highways. Where noise is an issue, the use of mechanical ventilation and cooling allows occupants to keep the windows shut. The following measures can be used for non-critical situations in which a designer is looking for the best sound insulation.

Window Type: Reduce sound transmission by adding more panes, heavier-than-air gas fills, such as argon and krypton, airtight window frames or thicker glass. (Different weights in each layer is best.) Fixed windows provide better sound isolation than operable ones. With a Sound Transmission Coefficient (STC) rating with a value 3 to 5 lower than an equivalent operable window, they will reduce sound levels by a third or more. Good sound isolation in windows is consistent with good thermal performance.

Window Location: Locate windows on walls facing away from the source of the noise. Angling the windows away from the source will also reduce noise transmission.

Sound Barriers: Trees, shrubs and fences reduce the noise reaching a building. However, they should not shade windows, especially in peak solar collecting hours.

Summary

• Casement and awning windows have less air leakage than sliders. Fixed windows have the lowest possible air leakage.

• Casements usually have the largest operable area, which means they offer better ventilation than other types of windows.

• Glass block is inappropriate for solar glazing because of its low SHGC and RSI values.

• High-performance windows placed flush with the outside wall surface provide increased solar gain and only marginally increased risk of condensation.

• To avoid sunlight passing directly through a space, do not locate windows at both sides of a corner.

• A south-facing bay window will have worse thermal performance than an ordinary window in a wall opening of the same size.

• When planning dormers, take into account the additional heat loss through the building envelope due to the extra roofing and walls.

• Do not use skylights for passive solar heating as they produce high heat gains and curb losses in summer. To minimize these losses, use insulated curbs and avoid skylights over attics that require large light-wells.

• Wood, vinyl and foam-filled fibreglass are good choices for window-frame material. They minimize energy use and reduce the potential for condensation.

• In well-insulated houses, heat loss through framing members can be significant. To reduce these losses, use fewer large windows, locate the windows to coincide with the stud spacing and insulate the rough window openings.

• To reduce condensation on windows, install higher-performance windows and control excessive humidity with mechanical ventilation.

• Higher-performance windows help avoid local thermal comfort problems.

• Window systems that gather the best daylight reduce the consumption of electric light over a large part of the year.

• Good seals and multiple panes can minimize sound transmission through windows, particularly if the windows are filled with argon or krypton.

Part 2
Design Integration and Strategies

6. Design Integration

Chapters 1 to 5 of this book presented the elements of passive solar design that designers and builders need to know to create comfortable, energy-efficient homes. These elements include the physical characteristics of solar energy as a resource; the collection, storage and distribution of solar energy; summer comfort; and the important role of windows. Chapter 6 brings it all together by explaining how to integrate these elements to create winning solar designs.

Interior Space Planning

The best arrangement of interior space is the one that takes maximum advantage of the sun's energy. When designing a passive solar home, consider how the rooms and spaces will be used at different times of the day and in different seasons. Construct a sun path diagram like the one shown in Figure 2.1, taking into account any external obstructions. Draw trial floor plans in the sun path chart to see if the sun's position compliments planned activities. The house design shown inside the sun path illustrates some of the concepts discussed below. A general rule for planning interior space is to locate areas in which there is a lot of activity to the south on the floor plan and less used areas to the north. The following are specific examples.

Kitchens: In most homes, a kitchen, especially when integrated with a dinette, is a high-activity area. Locating it to the south and east provides early morning sun at breakfast and avoids having to prepare the dinner-time meal on the warmer west side of the house.

Family and Living Rooms: A southerly location provides a pleasant daytime activity area, especially for young children. The normally large, open space and the connection with adjacent areas enhances heat storage and circulation.

Dining Rooms: Formal dining rooms are often used only occasionally and in the evening. Locate them to the north.

Bedrooms: A bedroom used as an office, playroom or studio should have a south location in preference to bedrooms used purely for sleeping.

Bathrooms: Because of their small size and infrequent use, bathrooms should be located on any other than a south face. An internal location is consistent with the need for privacy. Locating bathrooms internally can reduce plumbing costs and heat loss from long water lines. Another advantage is that an internal bathroom does not have windows on which humidity can condense.

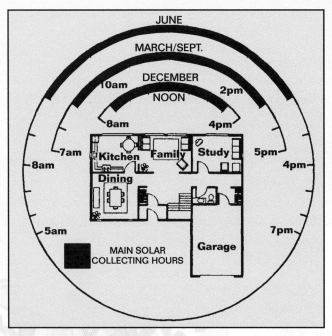

FIGURE 2.1 Sun path chart for space layout planning (45°N latitude)

Sunspaces: Locate sunspaces on the south side of the house and connect them to as many rooms as possible. Putting the sunspace inside the house rather than protruding from it will help achieve this and reduce heat losses. (See Figure 2.2.)

Utility Rooms: Locate closets, storage areas, the garage and other infrequently used rooms on the north side of the house where they act as buffer zones.

Basements: Increasing window areas in basements can make them into attractive living spaces.

Opening up the south wall with glass by creating a walk-out or localized depressed-grade area increases solar collection. In addition, the basement concrete floor can provide heat storage and improve the use of solar heat if the complete basement floor is insulated. The mass of the poured concrete or block walls adds nothing to the thermal mass of the space because they lie behind an insulated finished wall. Insulating on the outside of the wall and leaving the inside wall unfinished could provide thermal mass.

Using the basement for bedrooms instead of adding a second level is an economical approach. (See Design 5.) An added benefit is that the bedrooms are in the coolest part of the home.

Porches: Porches on the west side of the house provide useful shading of west-facing windows.

Study and Sewing Rooms: These rooms are best located on corners with windows on both exterior walls to give high daylight levels, even light distribution and minimum glare.

Balconies: A balcony offering a private outdoor space above grade can shade the room below it during the summer. To avoid shading during the winter, limit the size of balconies over south-facing windows to the values given in Figure 1.26.

Floor Plans

Open floor plans are better than partitioned ones as they allow solar gains to circulate freely. In addition, two-storey compact plans are better than single-storey plans because they enhance air circulation. Where partition walls are needed for privacy, north-south partitions are preferable to east-west partitions because they allow north-south air circulation. They also provide effective heat storage since both sides of the wall receive solar radiation for one half of the day each.

Envelope Design

A passive solar home should conserve energy with a properly designed, well-insulated and airtight envelope. The requirements of the National Energy

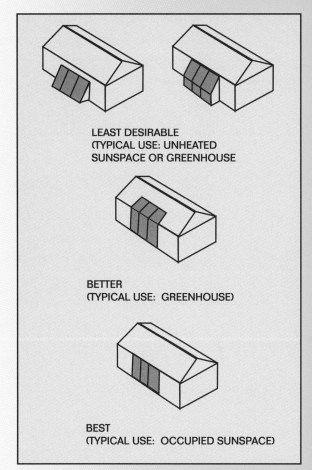

LEAST DESIRABLE
(TYPICAL USE: UNHEATED
SUNSPACE OR GREENHOUSE)

BETTER
(TYPICAL USE: GREENHOUSE)

BEST
(TYPICAL USE: OCCUPIED SUNSPACE)

FIGURE 2.2 Sunspace design options

Code for Houses (NECH) are the minimum. (The values are tabulated in Part 3.) Higher levels, such as those used in the R2000 house, are recommended.

Compact designs maximize energy efficiency and minimize envelope construction costs. For example, duplexes and row houses have lower heat losses than single-family dwellings; and square-plan, two-storey homes have lower heat losses than L-shaped bungalows. (See Figure 2.3.) As envelope components become better insulated, framing becomes the weak thermal link. Therefore, attention should be paid to minimizing thermal bridging.

Features such as bay windows, projections, convoluted floor plans and cathedral ceilings add character to a home but at an energy cost. Moreover, additional framing around windows and skylights increases thermal bridging. This is another reason for choosing fewer larger windows over several smaller ones. In addition, framing and roof curbs around skylights lower their thermal performance.

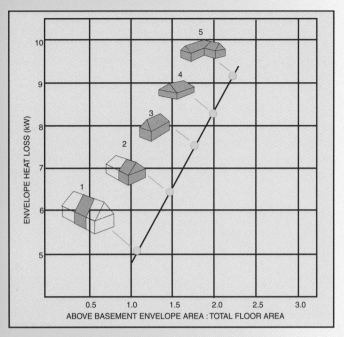

FIGURE 2.3 Effect of building form on heat loss

Values for a 150 m² dwelling, 20% glass-to-floor area, Ottawa, with envelope to 1995 NECH for gas heat

1. Townhouse
2. Semidetached
3. Detached two-storey
4. Bungalow
5. L-shaped bungalow

When planning the roof, consider the future use of solar collectors (hot water and photovoltaic). A 45°, south-facing slope is a positive compromise in most Canadian locations.

National Energy Code for Houses

The Model NECH acknowledges the benefit of south-facing windows and makes special allowances for their use. However, it does not fully recognize all the potential benefits of passive solar design. House designers should be aware of the limitations it imposes. The following is a brief overview of the Code and the key issues that affect passive solar design. The Model Code covers all dwellings up to and including small apartment buildings up to three stories high, with a footprint not exceeding 600 m².

It includes different categories of requirements. Mandatory requirements are required in all circumstances. Prescriptive requirements are required unless alternative measures would result in lower energy use. Showing equivalency using a computer analysis is the "Performance Compliance Path." A simpler subset of this is the "Trade-off Compliance Path" in which individual prescribed envelope characteristics can be traded off for others as long as the total consumption remains within the expected level.

The Code requirements are based on cost-effectiveness and vary with location and type of fuel. For example, dwellings with electric heating are required to have higher envelope insulation values and better windows than gas-heated homes. In most instances, they are also required to have heat recovery ventilation systems.

The following NECH considerations directly affect passive solar design.

• An unheated space, such as a sun porch or enclosed veranda, is only credited with increasing the common wall insulation value by RSI 0.16.

• The ratio of glass area to floor area should not exceed 20 percent. This window allowance is a generous figure that allows wide latitude for passive solar design. (All the designs in Part 3 have a total glass-to-floor-area ratio of less than 20 percent; the highest is 16 percent.)

• Recognizing the benefit of passive solar heating, only half of the glass facing within 45° of due south is counted. Windows must have an SHGC greater than 0.58 (see Figure 1.11) and be unshaded at noon on December 21; and the building must have an air-circulation system. (A normal furnace circulation system satisfies this requirement.) For partially shaded windows, the 50 percent rule explained in the NECH can be applied to the unshaded part. The benefit cannot be claimed if the building is air conditioned unless the glass is shaded by exterior devices at noon on June 21.

• There are minimum thermal performance requirements for windows, which are expressed in terms of Energy Rating (ER). These values vary with location and type of fuel used. For example, the Code requires a gas heated house in Vancouver to have operable windows with an ER value of (-24) and an electrically heated home in Winnipeg to have an ER value of (-6). (See Figure 2.4.)

A building not meeting the requirements must have an energy analysis using approved software. The software automatically compares the calculated energy consumption of the proposed design to the same building built to the prescriptive requirements.

The process does not give full credit to a number of passive solar design strategies discussed below. This does not mean, however, that the Code prohibits such strategies or that they are inappropriate, but only that no credit is given to them for the purpose of demonstrating compliance with the Code.

• Currently, HOT2000 is the only software approved for demonstrating compliance. This is a single-zone model that considers the house as one space and cannot calculate the impact of mass located in a remote area of the house.

• Unheated or partially heated sunspaces must be modelled as fully heated on the assumption that they may be provided with full comfort heating later.

• The effects of exterior shading are not accounted for.

• Heating systems must be modelled with a constant set-point temperature, and excess solar heat must be vented when the indoor temperature exceeds 24.5°C. The result is an underestimate of the potential solar contribution.

Mechanical Systems

An efficient heating, ventilating and, if necessary, air conditioning system complements a well-designed building envelope. The NECH's requirements for mechanical systems equipment should be considered the minimum, and higher-efficiency mechanical systems can often be very cost effective. The following are areas in which the selection and design of

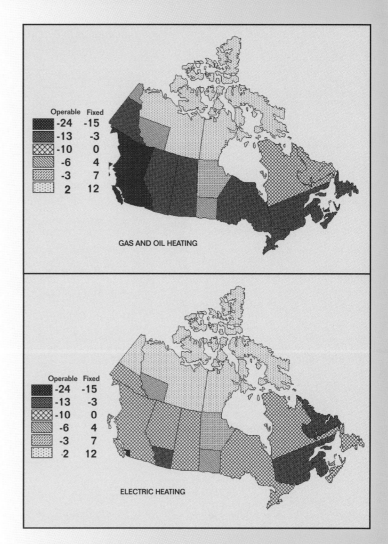

FIGURE 2.4 Minimum house window ER values, NECH

mechanical systems can affect passive solar design.

• Forced-air furnaces provide whole-house air circulation to distribute solar gains. However, if the furnace fan runs continuously, annual energy use will be high. Energy use will be lower if the fan is shut off in the summer and operates only when the south zone of the house becomes overheated.

The room thermostat that controls the heat should be located in the north side of the house, and the thermostat for the fan circulation should be located in the south (solar collecting) zone. Some furnaces have high-efficiency, electronically commutated (EC) motors that reduce energy consumption by up to 40 percent compared to conventional motors. Figure 2.5 gives typical fan costs for various operating strategies.

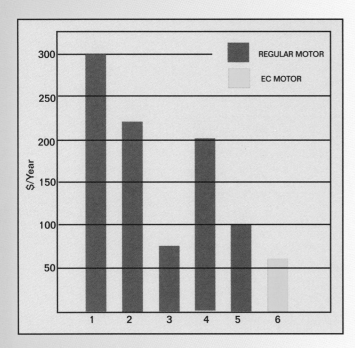

FIGURE 2.5 Approximate annual cost of various fan operating modes for typical 150-m² house (electricity @ 8.0¢ per kW h)

1. Fan runs all year
2. Fan runs during heating season
3. Fan cycles with demand for heating
4. Fan runs continuously on low speed; high speed on demand for heat
5. Fan cycles on demand for heat and solar heat distribution
6. Fan cycles on demand for heat and solar heat distribution, with high-efficiency EC motor

To even out the distribution of heat throughout the dwelling, use high-level return air grilles to recirculate the warm air that collects at the highest points in the house.

• When using radiant or baseboard heating, an air circulation method is required to distribute solar heat. Circulating the air to all habitable rooms is also a Code requirement for proper ventilation.

• Radiant heating systems can benefit rooms with large window areas by providing comfort at lower air temperatures. In well-insulated rooms and areas with windows having high ER values, lower air temperatures can be comfortable with conventional heating systems. Mass floors exposed to the sun should not have heating elements installed in them as this will limit the storage of solar heat.

• Use programmable set-back thermostats to get the best solar contribution. Determining the most appropriate set-back schedule involves trial and error since it depends on the weather, the heating system and the thermal mass of the dwelling. For example, it takes less time for a house to cool down and more time for it to warm up in mid-winter than in milder weather.

• Mechanical means of venting excess heat from sunspaces must be carefully designed to avoid creating negative pressures within the dwelling. Negative pressures can cause combustion gases to spill from fireplaces, furnaces and boilers that rely on natural draft. Ideally, all of the solar heat should contribute to house heating.

• As the airtightness and the insulation value of a window increase, the need to supply heat directly below the window decreases. With windows having an ER value above -10 in Vancouver, -5 in Ottawa and 0 in Winnipeg, it is safe to abandon this practice. This reduces the cost of duct work by locating registers more centrally and using shorter duct runs. (See Design 4.)

Interior Acoustics

The hard, uncovered surfaces that provide maximum heat storage, and the wide, open spaces that promote air circulation, are not the best for aural privacy and low reverberation within a dwelling. Multiple-pane, gas-filled windows and well-insulated walls will reduce exterior noise transmission. The following are measures that can improve internal acoustics while reducing any adverse effect on solar contribution:

• Provide sound-absorbing furnishings, such as rugs, where they will not shade mass floors.

• Use heavy drapes. They are good sound absorbers and will not inhibit solar gains if parked clear of the window.

• Arrange for the air to circulate through traffic routes or family activity areas rather than private quiet spaces.

• Provide oversized or double doors that can be closed when privacy is required.

Air Quality

Many passive solar design strategies can also improve the quality of a home's indoor air. The following suggestions will to help reduce indoor air contaminants.

• Avoid carpets. Harder flooring provides better solar heat storage and reduces outgassing, dust and mould. Choose cement mortar over petroleum-based products when selecting adhesives for tile floors.

• Use lots of natural light throughout the house to sustain healthy plant growth. Many plants are good for reducing air pollutants.

• Provide good air circulation to minimize stagnant areas and mould growth.

• Select high-performance windows to eliminate the risk of mould caused by condensation around the edges of the frame and sill.

Orientation and View

When a choice of building orientation is possible, there may be a conflict between the best solar orientation and the best view. If this is the case, create a view with careful landscaping to the south of the dwelling. This allows you to follow passive solar heating guidelines. If this is not possible, consider the following solutions.

• Minimize the glass area in the direction of the view and locate windows to give the best possible view.

• For northerly views, it is more important to limit heat loss through the window than to collect solar heat. Therefore, high RSI values are more important than high SHGC values.

• For east and west views, high RSI values are more important than high SHGC values. It is better to use low SHGC windows to avoid overheating in the summer unless there is adequate shading.

Where the south side of the house faces the street, large window areas can reduce privacy. To address this problem, maintain a good distance from the sidewalk and introduce an eye-level fence or hedge. Another solution is to relocate the principal activity areas towards the back of the house. Glass block is a good choice for a partition between front and back because it transmits light and serves as thermal mass. Stopping the partition before the ceiling, or allowing for an opening, helps maintain air circulation.

Fabric Fading

Low-e coatings reduce the transmission of ultraviolet light. This, in turn, lessens but does not necessarily eliminate fabric fading, which is proportional to the intensity of light and the amount of exposure to it. Only by decreasing the amount of incoming light can fading be significantly reduced. High temperatures, humidity and air impurities also hasten fading. Rooms that are constantly sunlit should be furnished with this in mind.

Colour Finishes

Heavyweight room surfaces, such as concrete and brick, that serve as thermal mass can be almost any colour, but dark matte surfaces are slightly better. It is best to finish lightweight elements with light matte surfaces because light surfaces redistribute solar heat to other surfaces and increase daylight levels. Matte surfaces also prevent reflections that can cause glare.

Do not finish window walls in dark colours that increase visual discomfort when viewed against a bright window. However, dark matte-finish floors can limit the glare caused by reflected sunlight without significantly affecting daylight levels. They also show less dirt than light floors.

The texture of the surface is actually more important than its colour. A rough surface that feels non-slip to the touch will absorb most of the radiation that falls on it, regardless of its colour. Whether it is used in walls, such as fireplace or feature walls, or in floors, mass should have a rough surface. Brick, concrete block, non-ceramic tile, stone and poured concrete all have the required roughness for good absorption of solar radiation. They are also usually non-white, which makes them suitable in terms of colour as well.

Household Appliances

As insulation levels increase, the heat generated by lights and household appliances can meet an increasing proportion of a home's heating needs, thereby reducing potential solar contribution. Using energy-efficient lights and appliances can reduce the generated heat by as much as 50 percent. The reduction of these internal gains will be replaced partially by solar gains and partially by the heating system. This will result in lower energy use and higher solar contribution. Figure 2.6 compares the typical energy consumption of conventional and high-efficiency appliances.

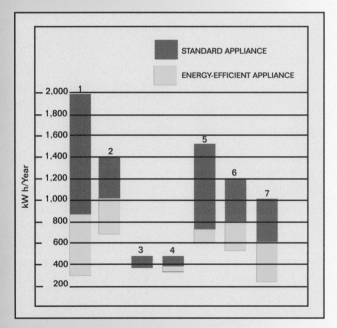

FIGURE 2.6 Comparison of annual electrical energy use of standard and high-efficiency appliances

1. Refrigerator
2. Dishwasher
3. Range
4. Oven
5. Clothes washer
6. Clothes dryer
7. Lighting

Design Evaluation Using Computers

Computer modelling is a valuable way to gain experience and improve house designs. It allows the designer to try out several ideas on a single plan and get instant feedback. This is critical when considering new technologies and products. However, no computer program is sophisticated enough to allow designers to study the interaction among all the elements of passive solar design. The programs available tend to be bound to traditional design disciplines, such as architecture, structural and mechanical engineering, and cost estimating.

For designers interested in getting the most energy efficiency from a house, thermal models can make the task easier. While the guidelines in this book will help steer the design in the right direction, they will not account for all the possible variations and details. This can be done with thermal modelling. The following thermal models are suitable for the analysis of dwellings.

HOT2000: HOT2000 is targeted specifically at residential buildings. Its key features are:

• calculations based on average monthly data (Bin Method);

• modelling of thermal bridging through stud walls;

• a detailed air infiltration model;

• basement and foundation modelling based on National Research Council (NRC) test results; and

• a detailed window model.

HOT2000 has been approved for demonstrating compliance with the National Energy Code for Houses. Extensive field monitoring of actual houses has confirmed its accuracy as a design tool.

ENERPASS: ENERPASS is a multi-zone thermal model that performs hourly calculations using heat transfer equations. It also offers a simplified daylight analysis and is well-suited to modelling residential and small, commercial, high-solar-use buildings. Its features include:

• up to seven thermal zones with infiltration air exchange possible between zones;

• accurate solar ray tracing;

• detailed NRC Basement model;

• modelling of most residential and small, commercial heating, ventilation and air conditioning systems;

• calculation of all energy flows, including space heating and cooling, domestic water heating, lighting, fans and appliances; and

• design-day calculation for equipment sizing.

ENERPASS was developed in Canada by Enermodal Engineering in Waterloo, Ontario. The company fully supports the program and offers a consulting service for designers who do not wish to carry out their own analysis. The program can also be custom-modified to simulate almost any other building feature or system, except shading from adjacent buildings. The accuracy of this software has been validated.

Energy Targets and Solar Contribution

Energy Targets: To judge the effectiveness of a proposed design, designers need benchmarks. Figure 2.7 provides benchmarks for target energy consumptions in three locations. They represent the annual space-heating achievable for plain, compact homes constructed according to the NECH. Two sets of targets are shown: one for housing built to insulation levels and window ER values required for electric heating; the other as required for gas heating.

Since energy usage per unit of area depends on house size, the targets will be more difficult to meet for smaller-than-average homes. (Targets were calculated for a 180-m² detached home, a 130-m² semidetached home, and a 116-m² middle row house.)

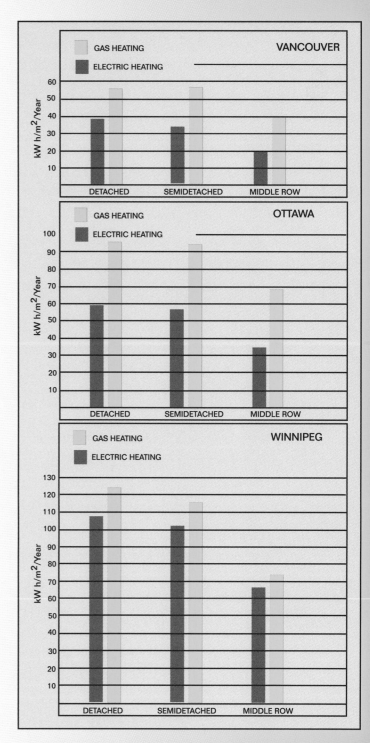

FIGURE 2.7 Net space-heating targets for energy-efficient housing

It is easy to achieve the targets by using higher insulation levels and higher-performing windows than needed. Many homes, such as R2000 houses, have been built with envelopes better than these minimum requirements. For example, the pilot houses from the Advanced House Program all have significantly higher R-value envelopes than required by the Code, as well as annual energy consumption between 36 and 63 percent of the targets. Three of the designs (4, 5 and 6) presented in Part 3 are from the Advanced House Program.

Solar Contribution: In addition to overall performance, designers often want to see how effectively they have applied the techniques of passive solar heating. A simple way of doing this is the Solar Fraction method. The Solar Fraction is given for each house design in Part 3.

This value is equal to the ratio of the useful solar gains to the home's annual heating consumption, calculated as if these gains were not present. The higher the Solar Fraction, the greater the solar energy used. Even modestly glazed homes can expect Solar Fractions of about 25 percent. The figure can rise to 50 percent or more in homes with the best windows in more temperate parts of the country.

However, higher Solar Fractions do not necessarily mean lower purchased energy usage. The heat loss could rise along with the Solar Fraction enough to more than offset the solar gains. Only a thermal analysis will show the trend.

Summary

• Arrange interior spaces to make the best use of the sun's energy by considering how rooms will be used at different times of the day.

• Compact, two-storey designs are minimum-envelope, minimum-energy solutions. Open plans improve air circulation and the use of solar energy; internal partitioning should run north-south.

• If a window area beyond that allowed by the NECH is proposed, computer models can demonstrate that the proposed design will match the expected level of performance.

• Install mechanical systems and equipment with efficiencies above those specified in the NECH.

• Forced-air furnaces provide a ready means of distributing solar gains. To reduce energy consumption, operate the furnace fan intermittently and on demand for heat and solar heat distribution.

• Higher-performance windows eliminate the need to locate heat outlets below windows.

• Passive solar design and better indoor air quality are complementary goals.

• Where windows cannot be oriented for maximum solar benefit, limit the window areas and choose windows with high insulation values.

• Where overheating is a risk, use shading or windows with a low SHGC.

• Use light matte finishes for interior surfaces except heavyweight elements and floors.

• A rough texture on a surface is more important for storing heat than its colour.

• Energy-efficient appliances reduce internal heat gains and create greater opportunity to use solar energy.

• The higher the Solar Fraction, the greater the solar energy used.

7. Site Planning and House Design Strategies

As explained in Chapter 6, good passive solar design works in harmony with other aspects of planning a house, such as the use of interior space, mechanical systems, the quality of the indoor air and acoustics. Chapter 7 integrates other issues that architects and builders must consider as part of any passive solar strategy. It focuses on site planning, direct-gain systems, sunspaces and design approaches for detached, semidetached and row housing.

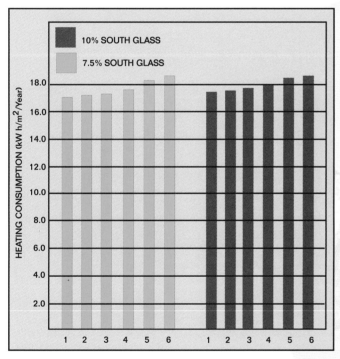

FIGURE 2.8 Effect of off-south orientation on house heating consumption

Figures are for an average-sized detached home in Ottawa with 2.5 percent glass-to-floor area, east, west and north

1. Home oriented due south
2. Home rotated 15° off south
3. Home rotated 30° off south
4. Home rotated 45° off south
5. Home rotated 60° off south
6. Home rotated 75° off south

Site Planning For Solar Access

Whether siting a home on a single property or planning a subdivision, the basic rules remain the same: keep the south side of the house unshaded during the winter and plan it to accommodate large window areas. However, the windows do not need to face directly south to provide useful solar gain. There is practically no loss of performance if the glass is within 15° of true south. In fact, orientations up to 25° or 30° off due south, while less effective, can still provide substantial solar gains. (See Figure 2.8.)

In subdivisions, streets with an east-west orientation provide the best opportunity for solar access. This need not be due east-west. Orientations off by up to 30° generate acceptable solar collection while accommodating other design considerations, such as natural grades, the street layout and view.

Figure 2.9 illustrates typical shadow patterns cast by a two-storey dwelling at the winter solstice and at the spring and fall equinoxes (about March 21 and September 21, respectively). The figure is scaled to represent a latitude of 45°N.

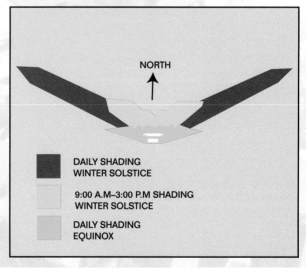

FIGURE 2.9 Typical shadow patterns cast by a two-storey house, 45°N latitude

For the purposes of site planning, designers need to consider only shadows at the winter solstice, because shadows are shorter at all other times of the year. Early morning and late evening shadows are not a concern as there is little heat in the solar radiation at these times. A full 99 percent of the daily solar gains through a south window at 45°N occurs between 9:00 a.m. and 3:00 p.m. at the winter solstice. This figure drops to 78 percent between 10:00 a.m. and 2:00 p.m.

Figure 2.10 shows the shadow patterns produced between 9:00 a.m. and 3:00 p.m. superimposed on a typical subdivision lot. Figure 2.11 gives variations of shadow length with latitude and site-slope for typical one- and two-storey dwellings. Some overlap of shadow and house plan can be accepted without significant reduction of solar gain. The actual acceptable overlap depends on the height of the window sill since shading of the wall below the window has no significant influence on solar gains.

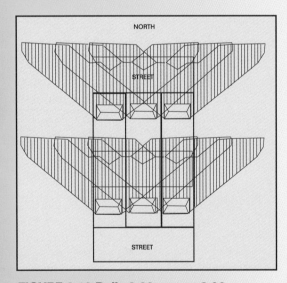

FIGURE 2.10 Daily 9:00 a.m. to 3:00 p.m. shadow patterns at the winter solstice, typical subdivison for 45°N latitude

A low-pitched or mansard-type roof that reduces the effective height of a building can reduce shadow lengths. To maintain solar-ready roofs (for domestic water heating or photovoltaic cells), use a compound-pitch roof with the south-facing side inclined at 45°.

Where overshadowing is unavoidable, raise the height of the window sill to minimize shading of the window. If windows are subjected to long periods of overshadowing, reducing their size will lower overall heat loss.

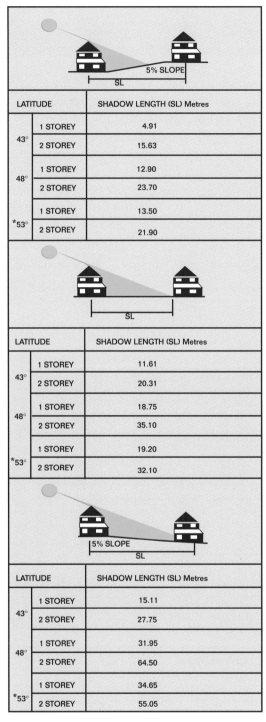

LATITUDE		SHADOW LENGTH (SL) Metres
43°	1 STOREY	4.91
	2 STOREY	15.63
48°	1 STOREY	12.90
	2 STOREY	23.70
*53°	1 STOREY	13.50
	2 STOREY	21.90

LATITUDE		SHADOW LENGTH (SL) Metres
43°	1 STOREY	11.61
	2 STOREY	20.31
48°	1 STOREY	18.75
	2 STOREY	35.10
*53°	1 STOREY	19.20
	2 STOREY	32.10

LATITUDE		SHADOW LENGTH (SL) Metres
43°	1 STOREY	15.11
	2 STOREY	27.75
48°	1 STOREY	31.95
	2 STOREY	64.50
*53°	1 STOREY	34.65
	2 STOREY	55.05

FIGURE 2.11 Shadow lengths at winter solstice for a number of latitudes and site grades

*For 53°N, 10:00 a.m. – 2:00 p.m. shadow length is reported. For 43°N and 48°N, 9:00 a.m. – 3:00 p.m. shadow lengths are reported

Direct-gain Strategies

The simplest and most cost-effective solar strategy is direct gain. In a direct gain system, sunlight enters the room and heats it; mass in the room absorbs excess solar heat; and air circulation distributes the heat to other rooms. This strategy calls for no special design. A conventional house with sensible window placement and good internal air circulation can be a direct-gain system. In fact, all houses can benefit from improved solar performance by adopting this simple strategy.

Sun Tempering: Sun tempering can be a normal part of every house design by using modest areas of south-facing glass (6 to 10 percent of the floor area).

High Solar Fraction: As the area of south-facing glass is increased, steps must be taken to make full use of the additional solar gains and to prevent overheating. Careful analysis is required. While south-facing glazing is important in all passive solar heating strategies, it does not need to face directly south.

When laying out the building, use true south rather than magnetic (i.e., compass) south. Keep in mind that a building facing east of south is better in terms of solar gain than one facing west of south because the early morning sun entering the east windows helps to warm the house from its setback temperature. East windows also cause less overheating than west windows, where afternoon solar gains coincide with higher ambient air temperatures.

As the window area is increased, less of the solar gain is fully used unless deliberate design measures are taken. (Figure 2.12 shows typical relationships.) Increasing the glass area reduces space heating to a minimum, beyond which it starts to rise again, because solar gains cannot be effectively used (Point A). The best design solution would be the one at which Point A coincides with an acceptable level of overheating hours.

If overheating hours are excessive, the glass area can be reduced or thermal mass added. Assuming that the maximum acceptable number of hours over 26°C is 20, the correct percentage of glazing for the house design would be Point B (8.75 percent south glass). The best glazing solution will vary with the building's design and location and should be checked by analysis.

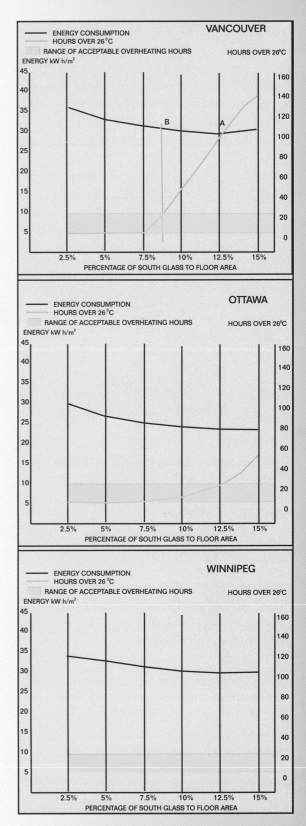

FIGURE 2.12 Typical variation of space heating and overheating hours with south glass area

Data is for conventional wood-frame, single-detached houses built to the thermal requirements for gas heat in the NECH. Overheating hours are counted for the months of November through March

47

Sun-tempered Design

• There should be no more that 8 percent south-facing glass unless a thermal analysis is being done. The percentage of south-facing glass area at which overheating occurs will vary according to the dwelling's location and envelope design.

To have a higher percentage of south-facing glass without the risk of overheating, install triple or quadruple low-e windows. (They have a lower SHGC than double windows.) In cold locations, such as Winnipeg, even with clearer skies, up to 10 percent south glass area should be acceptable if triple or quadruple low-e windows are used.

• Distribute the windows evenly among south-facing rooms.

• East, west and north window areas should be either the minimum permitted by Code or sufficient to meet daylighting and viewing needs.

• Good solar transmission is most important for south-facing glass and less so for north-facing windows. For east and west windows, shading may be required to avoid overheating.

• Provide air circulation of not less than three air changes an hour. A conventional furnace should have sufficient capacity to do this. To minimize electricity use, cycle the fan by means of a cooling-action thermostat located in the solar-collecting zone.

High Solar Fraction

• Limit the area of south-facing glass to 15 percent of the floor area.

• East, west and north windows should be either the minimum permitted by Code or sufficient to meet daylighting and viewing needs.

• Good solar transmission is most important for south-facing glass and less so for north-facing windows. For east- and west-facing windows, shading may be required to avoid overheating.

• For each additional square metre of south-facing window beyond that recommended for sun-tempered designs, add 6 m² of mass within the direct-gain space. Concentrate the mass in the areas that get the most sunlight.

• Provide exterior shading for summer comfort.

• Delay or eliminate the need for air conditioning by using enhanced ventilation systems.

• Check the proposed design using a suitable thermal model to ensure year-round comfort.

Sunspaces

Sunspaces are a sought-after feature in houses. They offer a bright, warm, sunny room and a pleasant spot during long, cold winters. This perception of the sunspace is often accompanied by the expectation that it reduces the energy consumption of the house to which it is attached. This is not the case unless it is designed and used with great care. In fact, add-on heated sunspaces always increase the dwelling's overall energy use.

A sunspace is a direct-gain space separated by a common wall from the main dwelling. The separation is important because without it the sunspace becomes part of the main dwelling. The common wall isolates the sunspace from the main dwelling. In fact, an attached sunspace is commonly referred to as an isolated-gain (i.e., indirect-gain) strategy.

This isolation allows the conditions in the sunspace to differ from those in the main house. Hence, the sunspace can function as a solar collector, a greenhouse for plants or a space for occasional use by people. Sunspaces can be designed to accommodate a combination of uses but not to fully satisfy all three. Figure 2.2 (page 40) illustrates some typical sunspace designs.

Sunspaces as Solar Collectors: A sunspace designed as a solar collector offers little opportunity for occupancy because of its extreme temperature swings.

The following design elements are important for good performance.

• The sunspace must not be heated.

• The common wall must be insulated to the same standard as the exterior walls. A masonry wall is recommended for thermal storage.

• The common wall should have doors or windows to allow natural air circulation to transfer excess heat to the main house. High and low openings are best, and they must be closeable to prevent heat loss from the house during evenings and on cold overcast days.

• A fan should automatically circulate warm air from the sunspace to the rest of the house. It should operate when the temperature in the sunspace is higher than that in the main dwelling, and the air should be vented from the top of the sunspace, where it is warmest. Multiple-speed or variable-speed fans controlled in relation to the temperature difference between the sunspace and the main house are the best.

• Incorporate a way to exhaust excess heat. In unvented sunspaces, temperatures can exceed 40°C even in winter.

• Choose the windows primarily for high transmission (i.e., high SHGC).

• A tight enclosure helps to control energy loss through infiltration.

• Elements with high thermal capacity increase the use of solar energy. An insulated slab-on-grade floor is a practical solution.

• The best window angle for maximum solar gains in winter is 10-15° greater than the site latitude. A good compromise is 45°. If angled windows are used, they should have summer shading or large openable areas.

• The floor areas should be as small as practicable. A large floor area means more losses through the enclosing envelope.

Sunspaces as Greenhouses: A sunspace designed as a greenhouse is dramatically different from a sunspace designed as a solar collector. At all times, the conditions in the greenhouse must be maintained within limits tolerable to plants, with the limits varying for different types of plants. The absolute minimum temperatures are 2°C for cool house plants, 7°C for temperate house plants and 13°C for hot house plants. (See Table 2.1.) A day-to-night temperature swing of 5-8°C is desirable.

A temperature of 32°C can harm many plants, and only a few plants like temperatures in excess of 29°C. To maintain these conditions, prevent high temperatures and achieve good thermal performance, the following design considerations are critical:

• Maintain a minimum daytime temperature of 5-10°C for cool houses; 10-13°C for temperate houses; and 13-18°C for hot houses. Temperatures between 20°C and 25°C are usually required for the propagation of seeds and cuttings.

• Provide for a heating system, such as baseboard heating, that is separate from the heating system for the main house.

• For a cool house, insulate the common wall to the same level as the exterior walls. For a temperate house, reduce the insulation. For a hot house, omit it altogether.

• Have closeable openings in the common wall.

• Design a means to exhaust excess heat from the greenhouse. Use either fans or operable vents, that operate automatically. A ventilation fan should provide about 20 to 40 air changes an hour. For natural ventilation, the vent area should be equal to one sixth of the floor area, with vents at high and low levels.

• Use a circulating fan to prevent the layering of hot air at the top of the greenhouse and to distribute it evenly.

• Use a fan to transfer excess heat to the main dwelling, taking care not to transfer excess humidity, odours and insects.

Plant Name	Light			Heat		
	Lo (3)	Med (4)	Hi (5)	Cool	Temperate	Warm
Aloe		•			•	
Aphelandra (Zebra Plant)		•				•
Araucaria (Norfolk Island Pine)		•		•		
Aspidesra	•			•		
Bougainvilla		•		•		
Camellia	•			•		
Chrysanthemum		•		•		
Citrus		•		•		
Codiaeum (Crutons)		•				•
Crassula (Jade)		•			•	
Dieffenbachia	•					•
Ferns		•(1)			•	
Ficus	•(2)	•(2)	•(1)(2)			•
Maranta	•					•
Orchids		•(1)			•(2)	•(2)
Palms		•(1)		•(2)	•(2)	•(2)
Philodendron		•(1)			•	
Rhododendron and Azalea		•		•		
Schefflera (Umbrella Tree)		•		•		
Yucca			•	•		

TABLE 2.1 Preferred growing conditions for a number of common house plants

Notes:
(1) Indirect light preferred
(2) Depends on specific plant
(3) 0-2 h sunlight; 1,000-1,500 lx daily illuminance
(4) 2-3 h sunlight; 1,500-2,500 lx daily illuminance
(5) 5 h sunlight; 2,500-3,500 lx daily illuminance

• Install insulating windows with high transmission characteristics. Multiple-pane, coated and gas-filled units are suitable and economical choices for warmer houses in colder climates, especially if high humidities are needed.

• Insulate the walls and roof of the sunspace to equal or better the minimum NECH requirements.

• Ensure that the structure is airtight to minimize heat and humidity losses.

• Increase solar use and limit temperature swings by incorporating high-mass floors and walls.

• The best window angle to achieve the lowest energy consumption is latitude plus 10-15°. Lower angles increase overheating; greater angles reduce overheating but at the expense of useful solar collection.

• Include top and side windows to maintain even plant growth.

• Summer shading is essential, and external, manually operated roller blinds are a good solution. Removable shading washes that are either sprayed or brushed on are another efficient way of blocking summer heat gains while providing sufficient daylight.

• Use a humidifier to help maintain winter humidity above 35 percent, although transpiration from the plants might be sufficient to sustain this level. (The preferred range for most plants is 40-75 percent relative humidity.)

Sunspaces as Sunrooms: Occupied sunspaces fall between the two previous types in terms of thermal performance. While their temperature variations need to be limited, they do not need to be controlled as closely as they do in greenhouses. The following design considerations will ensure good performance:

- Locate windows only on the south wall.

- Avoid sloping windows except for daylighting. Angled windows cause overheating. Vertical windows readily shed snow, stay cleaner and are more watertight.

- Insulate the walls and roof to NECH levels or higher.

- Follow airtight construction practices.

- Use insulating windows. Multiple-pane, coated and gas-filled units extend the useable hours of the sunspace without heating. They also cut down on condensation as nighttime temperatures drop in the sunspace.

- Insulate the common wall like an exterior wall.

- Do not heat the sunspace. This would extend its use but increase the home's energy consumption.

- If heating is provided to extend the use of the sunspace, the heating system must be separate from that of the main dwelling. Use a quick-response radiant system that can be fired up only when the space is being occupied. A sealed-combustion gas fireplace would be a suitable choice.

- If plants are to be grown in the space, choose cool types and provide heat only to prevent damage, or move the plants to the main house in colder weather.

- Install operable windows or doors in the common wall to allow natural air circulation to transfer excess heat to the rest of the house.

- Use an automatic fan to vent heat to benefit the main dwelling.

- Include operable or removable windows for summer ventilation. Removable windows can be replaced by bug screens for summer use.

- Incorporate shading, preferably external.

- Include high-mass floors and walls to limit temperature swings and increase the use of the solar heat.

Attached Dwellings

Duplexes, row housing and stacked units can all benefit from the adoption of passive solar heating principles.

Semidetached Homes: These homes have lower heat losses and less infiltration than similar-sized single-family homes because they have one less outside wall through which to lose heat. In such houses, the masonry of the common wall can be used as thermal storage if it is finished with wet plaster rather than strapping and drywall.

Windows on the end walls will contribute to overheating, particularly on the west side of the building. If east- or west-facing windows are not included, it is possible to use a higher ratio of glass to floor area in the south wall without overheating. Between 9 and 11 percent is a safe range.

The following guidelines will help achieve the best thermal performance.

- If the dividing walls are solid masonry with wet plaster, follow the high Solar Fraction guideline: six square metres of mass in the direct-gain space for each square metre of south-facing glass greater than the recommended safe percentage.

- East and west elevations may need to be different. For pairs of homes with an east-west orientation, the window area on the west elevation should not exceed 2 percent of the floor area, and the window area on the east elevation should not exceed 4 percent.

- Avoid pairs of homes with a north-south orientation. They offer little opportunity for solar use.

- If both units combined are as close as possible to a square floor plan or a cube, there will be minimum envelope surface and the lowest energy consumption.

Row and Stacked Units: The middle units of row and stacked housing have even lower envelope losses than a similar-sized semidetached home. In such units, less south-facing glass is needed to satisfy heating requirements, while the absence of east- and west-facing windows reduces the risk of overheating. Using plastered masonry for the common walls provides additional mass for greater solar use.

The following are additional guidelines for achieving maximum thermal performance in row and stacked units.

• Blocks of units should run east-west. Avoid "L," "U" and "T" configurations as they create unwanted shading.

• Treat end units the same as semidetached units (see above).

• Narrow, deeper units produce the most compact blocks with the lowest envelope area and the lowest energy use, but they also limit the area available for windows.

• A similar percentage of glass area as in detached homes can be used without the risk of overheating.

• To increase summer ventilation, choose casement windows that provide 100 percent opening for the north face, and use screen doors. Other options include operable clerestory windows and whole-house fans.

• For stacked units of wood construction, add a layer of poured concrete over the wood sub-floor to provide additional thermal mass. This allows the use of extra south-facing glass, improves fire integrity and reduces noise transmission.

• Arrange balconies for the units on the upper level to provide summer shading for the south-facing glass in the units below.

Summary

• The basic rule in site planning for solar access is keep the south side of the house unshaded during the winter and plan it to accommodate large areas of windows.

• When planning the site, consider only the shadows at the winter solstice. Shadows at other times of the year are shorter.

• A conventional house with sensible window placement and good internal air circulation can be a direct-gain system.

• For sun-tempered design, the amount of south-facing glass should be about 8 percent of the floor area. The amount of south-facing glass that causes overheating will vary according to the home's location and envelope design.

• A sunspace can be a solar collector, a greenhouse or a place for occasional use by people, but not all three.

• Attached dwellings such as semidetached homes can have a higher glass-to-floor area ratio in the south wall without overheating.

• In row and stacked housing, blocks of units should run east-west. Avoid "L," "U" and "T" configurations as they create shading.

8. Designing For Occupant Comfort

Occupant comfort is the ultimate criterion of success in integrating the many strategies of passive solar design. It is achieved by creating the right balance among the interacting elements of the house, such as window size and performance, window overhangs, conservation level, thermal mass and internal gains. This chapter defines the concept of occupant comfort and establishes guidelines to help the designer find the best mix of strategies to create it.

Comfort and Overheating

Two key variables define overheating:
- the discomfort temperature threshold; and
- the percentage of hours that exceed that threshold.

Because these are dependant variables, one of them must be fixed in order to facilitate analysis. Therefore, an overheating threshold of 4°C above the average heating season temperature for the house (approximately the thermostat setpoint) is used. This value is based on the thermal sensation scale, which, when evaluated for comfort, results in an acceptable band of 4°C above and below the desired temperature. Conditions outside that band are considered to be uncomfortable by 90 percent of people.

A survey of the occupants of six houses for which detailed monitoring information was available indicated overheating in homes where over 4 percent of the hours in a sunny period exceeded the overheating threshold temperature. (Four percent is about 30 hours in a one-month period. In the spring and fall, this is about 2 to 3 hours for each sunny day). Occupants in houses with 4 percent of the hours or less exceeding the threshold temperature reported no overheating.

Comfort Design Guidelines

Simulations using a typical 216 m² house (with a heated living space in the basement) led to the findings summarized in text, graphs and tables below. The graphs show the results of analysis for houses with specific characteristics and are indicative of trends only. They should not be used to provide exact numbers. A software program, *The Comfort Design Checker*, is provided to determine the recommended values for a new house. (See Appendix 2 for instructions on how to use it.)

• Critical Month

October is the critical month in the heating season for overheating. Although October and April are both nominally heating-season months with similar average temperatures, the temperature of the ground is lower in April, which results in heat loss. Further, clear-day, south-vertical solar heat gain is lower in April because of the higher sun angles. Finally, since the sun angles are the same in August and April, windows with overhangs are more likely to be at least partially shaded in April than October (since overhangs are used to reduce summer overheating in August).

• Conservation Level

The recommended south-facing, glazed area is highly dependant on the conservation level. (See Table 2.6 at the end of this chapter.) High conservation levels result in severe restrictions in the amount of south windows that can be used without excessive overheating. (See Figure 2.13.)

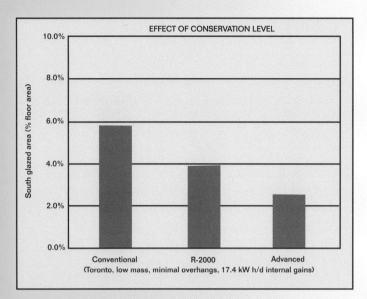

Figure 2.13 Effect of Conservation Level of Recommended Maximum South Glazed Area

Window Overhangs

Increasing the window overhang allows for additional south glazing. The ratio of eave-to-glass distance to overhang width is a critical factor affecting winter overheating. (See Figures 2.16, 2.17.)

Summer overheating is affected by the ratio of window height plus eave-to-glass distance to overhang width. Generally, July and August are the critical cooling months, with August being the most difficult to control in terms of passive solar heating because the sun angles are lower (i.e., they are equal to April).

• Thermal Mass

Adding more thermal storage mass allows more south glazing to be added without increasing overheating. However, at higher conservation levels, additional mass is slightly less effective in controlling overheating. (See Figure 2.14.)

Overhang Design Guidelines

As the south window area is increased, the proper design of the south window overhangs becomes critical to preventing overheating in the winter and summer.

You should design the overhang (the width from the glazing to the front of the overhang) and the eave-to-glass distance (the height of the bottom of

• Better Windows

Changing to more efficient glazing results in slightly less overheating (about 1 percent fewer hours in October). The increased thermal efficiency of the glazing has a smaller effect on building heat loss than on solar heat gain.

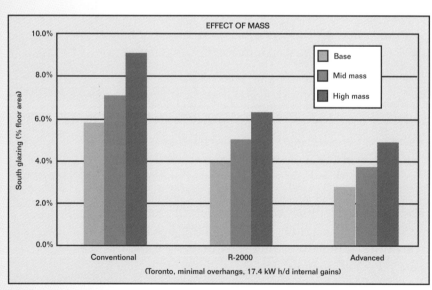

• Internal Gains

Assuming higher internal heat gains results in a significant reduction in the recommended south glazed area. (See Figure 2.15.)

Figure 2.14 Effect of Thermal Storage Mass on Recommended Maximum South Glazed Area for Three Typical Levels of Conservation

the overhang above the top of the glass) so that the sun just touches the top of the glazing at about 11:00 a.m. in October. This will ensure minimal shading from 10:00 a.m. to 2:00 p.m. (approximately 70-90 percent of insolation) from October through February — five of the seven space heating months. (See Table 2.2.) Using a larger eave-to-glass distance or a shorter overhang results in less shading in the other two space heating months (March and April) and more summer overheating because August and April have the same sun angles.

To reduce summer overheating, you should make the glazing short enough so that it would be fully shaded in August. However, this is practical only with clerestory glazings where a view is not needed. A less stringent requirement is to fully shade the glazing at noon on June 21st (see glass height + eave-to-glass distance in Table 2.2) at the expense of increased summer overheating or an increased summer cooling requirement.

Ideally, all south glazings should be optimally shaded by overhangs. With traditional "box" house designs, only the upper-floor glazings are shaded by the roof overhang. However, a number of design options allow for the shading of glazings on both floors. Examples include:

• shading the first floor windows with the roof overhang and the second-floor windows with dormers; and

• projecting the second floor out over the first-floor windows to create an overhang.

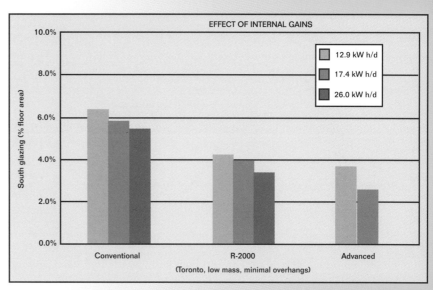

Figure 2.15 Effect of Internal Heat Gains on Recommended Maximum South Glazed Area for Three Typical Levels of Conservation

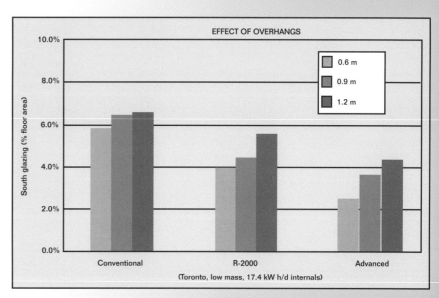

Figure 2.16 Effect of Overhang Width on Recommended South Glazed Area (0.3 m eave-to-glass distance in all cases)

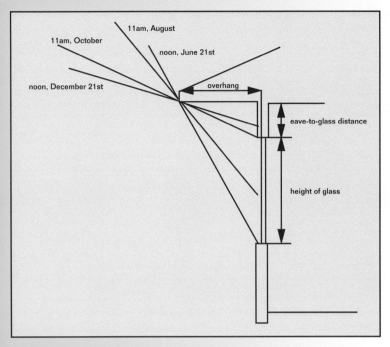

11am, August

11am, October

noon, June 21st

noon, December 21st

overhang

eave-to-glass distance

height of glass

Figure 2.17 Critical Sun Angle

Another approach is to determine the amount of shading for various predetermined glazing heights and overhangs, then select the configuration that best suits the design and construction requirements. (See Table 2.3.)

In general, the 0.3 m overhang with 0.2 m eave-to-glass distance, while not shading the south glazings in the winter, provides too little shading in the summer. The 1.2 m overhang with a 0.3 m eave-to-glass distance provides excellent shading in the summer but too much shading in the winter.

In most situations, the 0.6 m overhang with a 0.3 m eave-to-glass distance is a reasonable compromise. The 0.9 m overhang would be suitable for tall glazings, particularly at a high latitude. You can determine the shading performance of other overhang configurations with the *Comfort Design Checker* software.

		0.3 m overhang		0.6 m overhang		0.9 m overhang		1.2 m overhang[3]	
		Min. winter shading	Shade in June	Min. winter shading	Shade in June	Min. winter shading	Shade in June	Min winter shading	Shade in June
Latitude (degrees)	Cities in Latitude Range	Eave-to-glass distance[1]	Glass+ eave-to-glass distance[2]	Eave-to-glass distance	Glass+ eave-to-glass distance	Eave-to-glass distance	Glass+ eave-to-glass distance	Eave-to-glass distance	Glass+ eave-to-glass distance
		(m)	(m)	(m)	(m)	(m)	(m)	(m)	(m)
42 to 44	Toronto	0.2	0.8	glass distance	1.6	0.6	2.4	glass distance	3.3
44 to 46	Ottawa, Montreal, Halifax	0.2	0.7	0.4	1.5	0.6	2.2	0.8	3.0
46 to 48	St. John's, Moncton	0.2	0.6	0.4	1.3	0.6	2.0	0.7	2.7
48 to 50	Vancouver, Winnipeg	0.2	0.5	0.3	1.2	0.5	1.8	0.6	2.4
50 to 52	Calgary, Regina	0.2	0.4	0.3	1.1	0.5	1.7	0.6	2.2
52 to 54	Edmonton, Saskatoon	0.1	0.4	0.3	1.0	0.4	1.5	0.5	2.0

[1] Eave-to-glass distance needed to provide minimal shading between 10:00 a.m. and 2:00 p.m., October to February.

[2] Height from bottom of glazing to underside of overhang for glazing to be fully shaded on June 21st (38-45% shaded in August, Toronto to Edmonton, respectively (and locations between).

[3] This size of overhang can be achieved with a balcony or porch.

Table 2.2 Optimum Window Shading

(Values are approximate for range of latitude. More accurate values are available with the *Comfort Design Checker* software.)

Latitude (degrees)	Cities in Latitude Range	0.3 m overhang 0.2 m eave-to-glass distance		0.6 m overhang 0.3 m eave-to-glass distance		0.9 m overhang 0.3 m eave-to-glass distance		1.2 m overhang 0.3 m eave-to-glass distance	
		Winter shading	June shading	Winter shading	June shading	Winter shading	June shading	Winter shading	June shading
0.9 m window height									
42 to 44	Toronto	1%	68%	13%	100%	37%	100%	60%	100%
44 to 46	Ottawa, Montreal, Halifax	0%	61%	10%	100%	33%	100%	55%	100%
46 to 48	St. John's, Moncton	0%	52%	6%	100%	26%	100%	45%	100%
48 to 50	Vancouver, Winnipeg	0%	47%	4%	100%	23%	100%	42%	100%
50 to 52	Calgary, Regina	0%	41%	2%	94%	19%	100%	37%	100%
52 to 54	Edmonton, Saskatoon	0%	35%	0%	81%	14%	100%	30%	100%
1.2 m window height									
42 to 44	Toronto	1%	51%	10%	100%	27%	100%	45%	100%
44 to 46	Ottawa, Montreal, Halifax	0%	45%	8%	99%	25%	100%	41%	100%
46 to 48	St. John's, Moncton	0%	39%	4%	86%	19%	100%	34%	100%
48 to 50	Vancouver, Winnipeg	0%	35%	3%	78%	18%	100%	32%	100%
50 to 52	Calgary, Regina	0%	31%	1%	70%	14%	100%	28%	100%
52 to 54	Edmonton, Saskatoon	0%	26%	0%	61%	10%	100%	22%	100%
2.0 m window height									
42 to 44	Toronto	0%	31%	6%	66%	16%	100%	27%	100%
44 to 46	Ottawa, Montreal, Halifax	0%	27%	5%	61%	15%	96%	25%	100%
46 to 48	St. John's, Moncton	0%	23%	3%	52%	12%	85%	20%	100%
48 to 50	Vancouver, Winnipeg	0%	21%	2%	47%	11%	78%	19%	100%
50 to 52	Calgary, Regina	0%	19%	1%	42%	9%	71%	17%	100%
52 to 54	Edmonton, Saskatoon	0%	16%	0%	37%	6%	62%	13%	88%

Table 2.3 Location and Window Shading

Table 2.4 summarizes the simulation results in the recommended maximum south-glazing area for avoiding excessive solar overheating. It is based on:
- an eave-to-glass distance of 0.3 m;
- double or triple glazing plus one low-E coating; and
- a location in central Canada.

It provides a general and reasonable starting point for designing a house. The factors taken into the simulation are incorporated in the *Comfort Design Checker* software. These factors compensate for other values of internal gains, overhang dimen-

sions, glazing types and locations. The software program does everything needed to arrive at the suggested window sizes.

In Table 2.4, the recommended glazed area varies little from region to region (less than 1 percent). This is the result of the small variation in temperatures and clear-day insolation in the critical month of October among regions.

Table 2.5 shows approximate October, clear-day, 9:00 a.m to 6:00 p.m energy balances and full-day energy balances for a house with conventional construction and a relatively small amount of

Conservation Level	Internal gains kW h/day	Mass level*	0.6 m overhang	0.9 m overhang	1.2 m overhang**
			Maximum South-glazed Area (% floor area)		
Normal	26.0	Low	5.1	6.0	7.0
	26.0	Medium	6.3	7.1	7.8
	26.0	High	8.1	9.2	10.2
	17.4	Low	5.7	6.8	7.0
	17.4	Medium	6.5	7.6	8.5
	17.4	High	9.1	10.2	11.7
	12.9	Low	6.5	7.6	8.5
	12.9	Medium	8.2	9.2	10.4
	12.9	High	10.1	11.5	13.7
R-2000	26.0	Low	3.1	3.6	4.0
	26.0	Medium	3.6	4.1	4.6
	26.0	High	5.0	5.5	6.5
	17.4	Low	3.9	4.6	5.5
	17.4	Medium	4.9	5.6	6.5
	17.4	High	6.5	7.2	8.1
	12.9	Low	4.3	5.0	5.7
	12.9	Medium	5.3	6.1	6.9
	12.9	High	6.8	7.6	8.4
Advanced	17.4	Low	2.8	3.6	4.4
	17.4	Medium	3.6	4.5	5.3
	17.4	High	5.0	5.9	6.7
	12.9	Low	3.5	4.3	5.1
	12.9	Medium	4.6	5.4	6.3
	12.9	High	5.9	6.7	7.6

Table 2.4 Maximum South-glazed Area to Avoid Excessive Overheating

(Based on an eave-to-glass distance of 0.3 m, triple or double glazing plus one low-E coating; central Canada location.)

* Mass levels: **Low**—wood frame and gyproc, concrete basement
Medium—same as low but double gyproc.
High—same as medium plus a concrete topcoat on main floor and concrete, brick or stone walls equal
to at least six times the south-glazed area.

**This size of overhang can be created with a balcony or porch.

south glazing. Daytime gains exceed losses by a substantial but largely similar margin in all five cities. This similarity dictates comparable limits to glazing areas.

The following design features can enhance thermal comfort in a passive solar house:

• incorporating south-glazed areas and thermal storage into circulation areas to minimize heating of the occupant while heating the building (e.g., hallways and stairwells);

• distributing solar gains as deeply into the space as possible to minimize glare effects and maximize the use of thermal storage (e.g., locating windows near the north-south exterior or interior walls to allow the light to spread out over the wall surface);

	Vancouver 9 am–6 pm	Vancouver Day	Edmonton 9 am–6 pm	Edmonton Day	Toronto 9 am–6 pm	Toronto Day	Montreal 9 am–6 pm	Montreal Day	Halifax 9 am–6 pm	Halifax Day
Losses MJ	97	307	132	418	95	303	100	319	101	321
Gains:										
Internal MJ	23	63	23	63	23	63	23	63	23	63
Solar MJ	123	123	141	141	138	138	135	135	136	136
TOTAL MJ	146	186	164	204	161	201	158	198	159	199
Gains/Losses	151%	61%	124%	49%	169%	66%	158%	62%	157%	62%

Table 2.5 October, Clear-day Energy Balance

(Conventional house with 5 percent of floor area in south glazing and internal gains of 17.4 kW h per day.)

- locating glazing high in the walls (e.g., with clerestory windows) to distribute light and heat to the backs of the rooms and reduce occupant overheating;

- planning basements to make them brighter (more south glazing) and use the thermal storage capabilities of their floors and walls more fully;
- adding sufficient thermal storage to reduce temperature swings to acceptable levels. Examples include:
  - applying double gyproc
  - insulating the outside of the concrete in the basement (in addition to increased south glazing in basement)
  - applying a concrete topcoat on the floors (effective with tiled floors but relatively ineffective if floors are carpeted)

  - incorporating concrete, brick or stone "feature walls," particularly in highly glazed areas where the sun hits the wall directly
  - blowing warm air through ducted hollow concrete blocks, thereby using the inside of the blocks for thermal storage, either in floors or walls; and

- designing the mechanical system to distribute air to north rooms and between floors. This distributes excess heat in one area to the "thin mass" (gyproc, and so on) in areas with little or no south glazing.

	Above Grade:			Basement			
	Ceiling RSI	Walls RSI	Windows[1] RSI	Below-grade walls RSI	Floor perimeter RSI	Floor centre RSI	HRV[2]
Vancouver							
Conventional	5.8	2.3	0.4/0.5	0.8	none	none	No
R-2000	7.2	4.4	0.5/0.9	1.9	1.8	none	Yes
Advanced	10.0	4.4	0.9	1.9	1.8	1.8	Yes
Edmonton							
Conventional	7.2	3.1	0.5	0.8	none	none	No
R-2000	10.0	4.4	0.5/0.9	1.9	1.8	1.8	Yes
Advanced	10.0	4.4	0.9	2.9	1.8	1.8	Yes
Toronto							
Conventional	7.2	3.1	0.5	0.8	none	none	No
R-2000	7.2	4.4	0.5/0.9	1.9	1.8	none	Yes
Advanced	10.0	4.4	0.9	2.9	1.8	1.8	Yes
Montreal							
Conventional	7.2	3.1	0.5	0.8	none	none	No
R-2000	7.2	4.4	0.5/0.9	1.9	1.8	none	Yes
Advanced	10.0	4.4	0.9	2.9	1.8	1.8	Yes
Halifax							
Conventional	7.2	3.1	0.5	0.8	none	none	No
R-2000	7.2	4.4	0.5/0.9	1.9	1.8	none	Yes
Advanced	10.0	4.4	0.9	2.9	1.8	1.8	Yes

Table 2.6 Conservation Level Characteristics

Parametric hourly simulations were performed using Suncode on a house with 141.8 m² main and upper floor area and a 74.0 m² heated basement.

[1] Various window types for different scenarios

[2] Ventilation and infiltration: total 0.3 ac/h average for October

Part 3
Selected House Designs

About the 20 Sample Designs

This section of the book features 20 sample house designs. They were developed by Canadian architects and designers for specific Canadian cities. While each design makes deliberate use of the sun's energy to provide heat , it also meets a wide variety of needs, desires and budgets. The plans can be adopted directly, modified or viewed as a catalogue of ideas to help generate new designs.

For builders interested in offering passive solar housing, the designs include semidetached and townhouse versions in addition to detached homes. Some designs include features, such as bay windows, which conserve less energy than plain windows. This is not unusual as the house designs balance functionality, efficiency and cost with aesthetics.

Each design is presented in the following standard format.

About this Design: Provides an overview of the design, including its more interesting features.

Solar Features: Highlights features of the home which incorporate solar techniques. Unless otherwise noted, the designs have normal air circulation equal to that provided by a conventional furnace, and no added mass. Where the design includes south-facing bay windows, the south glass area includes the total bay window glass, not just the southern face.

Advance House Features: For designs from the Advanced House Program, the principal energy-conserving features are described.

Illustrations: The first illustration for each design presents the house as seen from the street. The illustrations lower on the page show additional details of the home's appearance, with notes on its solar features. Scaled floor plans and explanatory comments are also included. Basement floor plans are not shown unless a key part of the house design is located there. The scale for all floor plans is shown graphically.

Performance Table: Each design description contains a table showing the calculated energy performance of the house in three locations: Vancouver, Ottawa and Winnipeg. If one of these cities was the original design location, it is highlighted.

The annual energy use is given in kW h/m^2 of floor area (excluding unfinished basements). The values were calculated using the DOE energy analysis program.

Energy use has been calculated for houses with envelopes meeting the minimum thermal requirements of the 1995 NECH. Because these envelope requirements vary with the type of heating fuel used, the values for gas and electric heating options are reported separately.

Typical envelope constructions meeting these requirements are shown on the following pages. They are representative only, and other designs can be used to achieve similar insulation levels. As the advanced houses in the set show, using insulation levels higher than the Code minimums produces further reductions in energy use.

For the Advanced Housing Project designs, a third calculation using the actual values incorporated in the envelope construction has been made for the location closest to where the house was built.

The tabulated numbers provide a basis for comparing the heating costs for the different house designs. To get an estimate of the likely heating costs, multiply these figures by the floor area and the unit cost of fuel, then divide by the Seasonal Performance Factor of the heating system. Table 3.1 gives some typical values.

To convert kilowatt hours to the normal unit used for gas charges (cubic metres) divide by 10.4. For oil, divide the kilowatt hours by 11.6 to obtain litres. Calculating actual fuel costs based on annual consumption figures is problematic for fuels such as gas and electricity with monthly billings and a sliding rate tariff (i.e., the more you use, the lower the unit cost). In these cases, use an average unit cost of fuel. This information can usually be provided by the utility company or by using average figures from winter utility bills. A sample calculation is shown. The actual house consumption may vary from the tabulated numbers because of construction practices, occupant lifestyles, the severity of any given winter, and the modelling accuracy.

Solar Fraction: The last column in the Performance Tables reports Solar Fraction as defined on page 50. Table 3.2 summarizes the performance of the 20 designs. None of the houses analyzed indicated a potential overheating problem, the criteria for which is that the average above-grade indoor air temperature not exceed 26°C from November through to March.

Heating Systems and Fuel Type	Seasonal Performace Factors
GAS FURNACES	
• Conventional with electronic ignition	.68–.71
• As above with vent damper	.78–.80
• Power vented	.78–.80
• Condensing	.92–.80
OIL FURNACES	
• With flame retention head	.78–.80
HEAT PUMPS	
• Air source	1.5–2.2 [1]
• Water source	1.9–2.5 [2]
ELECTRIC HEATING	1.0

TABLE 3.1 Seasonal performance of common heating equipment

Notes:
(1) Location influences value
(2) Pumping energy influences value

SAMPLE CALCULATION
HOUSE DESIGN #1
OTTAWA

Case #1. Gas heat with condensing furnace with 0.94 Seasonal Performance Factor and gas cost of 25¢/m³.

Net heating required = 15,760 kW h
Gas consumption   = 15,760 kW h ÷ (0.94 x 10.4)
                   = 1,612m³

Gas heat cost   = 1,612 x 25¢/m³
                   = $403 per year

Case #2. Electric heat, electricity cost of 8¢/kW h

Net heating required = 9,730 kW h
Elec. comsumption   = 9,730 x 1.0 = 9,730 kW h

Electric heat cost = 9,730 x 8¢ /kW h
                    = $778.4 per year

Choosing a Plan

Selecting a house design can be complicated, and it is important to consider a host of factors other than energy performance. These include family size and needs, lifestyle, the cost of construction, appearance and special needs, such as accessibility. Before selecting a design, take the time to learn something about these other aspects. Not all the designs in this book will be suitable for all sites. For example, the size of units vary considerably from 116 to 256 m². Six are townhouses, five are semidetached and nine others are detached houses. All but one are designed for east-west streets. Some are designed for the north side of the street and others for the south. All are assumed to be free of shading from adjacent structures and landscaping.

When choosing a plan, remember that the designs can be easily and readily changed. The following are examples of possible modifications.

• The unit's dimensions can be changed to suit the lot.

• The level of passive solar contribution can be increased by making the south-facing opening bigger. Depending on the amount of the increase, extra mass may have to be added to avoid overheating in winter.

• The insulation levels and the window ER values can be increased. This will require a re-evaluation of the window areas.

• The window areas can be reduced or the windows relocated if there is significant shading or loss of privacy from neighbouring buildings.

The house designs presented here are ready to build but can be adjusted to meet the builder's or owner's unique needs. Whether your house is to be built "as is" or with modifications, have a professional prepare detailed working drawings before construction begins. These drawings are needed to obtain building permits and are essential to the proper building of the house. Finally, it is a good idea to do an energy analysis to refine the design following any significant change to the floor plan or design.

VANCOUVER GAS HEAT

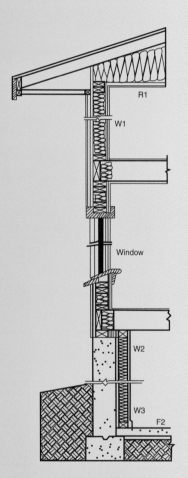

Assembly Code	Thermal Resistance of Illustrated Assembly (m² C°/W)	Required Thermal Resistance (NECH)	Components From Interior to Exterior
F2	1.08	1.08	• 100 mm concrete • Rigid insulation 25 mm
R1	7.13	7.20	• 13 mm gypsum board • Vapour barrier • 38 x 89 mm wood trusses @ 610 mm O.C. • Insulation 265 mm medium-density mineral fibre batts • Ventilated attic space
W1	3.83	3.40	• 13 mm gypsum board • Vapour barrier • 38 x 140 wood studs 406 mm O.C. • Insulation 140 mm low-density mineral fibre batts • Sheathing 29 mm semi-rigid glass fibre • Sheathing paper • Siding
W2	3.40	3.40	• 13 mm gypsum board • Vapour barrier • 38 x 89 mm wood studs @ 406 mm O.C. • Insulation 89 mm high-density mineral fibre batts • 38 mm EPS expanded polystyrene • 200 mm concrete
W3	3.23	3.10	• 13 mm gypsum board • Vapour barrier • 38 x 89 mm wood studs @ 406 mm O.C. • Insulation 89 mm high-density mineral fibre batts • 31 mm expanded polystyrene • 200 mm concrete
Window	Energy Rating of Window	Required Energy Rating (operable windows)	Window Description (all windows operable or with sash)
	-23	-24	• Double glazing • 12.7 mm air-gap • Low-e • Aluminum frame with thermal break

VANCOUVER ELECTRIC HEAT

Assembly Code	Thermal Resistance of Illustrated Assembly (m² C°/W)	Required Thermal Resistance (NECH)	Components From Interior to Exterior
F2	1.52	1.08	• 100 mm concrete • 33 mm rigid insulation
R1	8.72	7.20	• 13 mm gypsum board • Vapour barrier • 38 x 89 mm wood trusses @ 610 mm O.C. • 441 mm insulation loose-fill mineral fibre • Ventilated attic space
W1	3.83	3.40	• 13 mm gypsum board • Vapour barrier • 38 x 140 mm wood studs @ 406 mm O.C. • 140 mm insulation low-density mineral fibre batts • Sheathing 29 mm semi-rigid glass fibre • Sheathing paper • Siding
W2	3.40	3.40	• 13 mm gypsum board • Vapour barrier • 38 x 89 mm wood studs @ 406 mm O.C. • Insulation 89 mm high-density mineral fibre batts • 38 mm expanded polystyrene • 200 mm concrete
W3	3.40	3.10	• 13 mm gypsum board • Vapour barrier • 38 x 89 mm wood studs @ 406 mm O.C. • Insulation 89 mm high-density mineral fibre batts • 31 mm expanded polystyrene • 200 mm concrete
Window	Energy Rating of Window	Required Energy Rating (operable windows)	Window Description (all windows operable or with sash)
	-10	-10	• Double glazing • 12.7 mm argon-fill • Low-e • Vinyl frame

WINNIPEG GAS HEAT

Assembly Code	Thermal Resistance of Illustrated Assembly (m² C°/W)	Required Thermal Resistance (NECH)	Components From Interior to Exterior
F2	1.52	1.30	• 100 mm concrete • Rigid insulation 38 mm XTPs board type IV
R1	8.72	7.20	• 13 mm gypsum board • Vapour barrier • 38 x 89 mm wood trusses @ 610 mm O.C. • Insulation 441 mm loose-fill mineral fibre • Ventilated attic space
W1	3.83	3.00	• 13 mm gypsum board • Vapour barrier • 38 x 140 mm wood studs 406 mm O.C. • Insulation 140 mm low-density mineral fibre batts • Sheathing 29 mm semi-rigid glass fibre • Sheathing paper • Vinyl or aluminum siding
W2	3.23	3.00	• 13 mm gypsum board • Vapour barrier • 38 x 89 mm wood studs @ 406 mm O.C. • Insulation 89 mm high-density mineral fibre batts • 38 mm expanded polystyrene • 200 mm concrete
W3	3.40	3.10	• 13 mm gypsum board • Vapour barrier • 38 x 89 mm wood studs @ 406 mm O.C. • Insulation 89 mm high-density mineral fibre batts • 38 mm expanded polystyrene • 200 mm concrete
Window	Energy Rating of Window	Required Energy Rating (operable windows)	Window Description (all windows operable or with sash)
	-6	-6	• Triple glazing • 12.7 mm air-gap • Low-e • Wood frame

WINNIPEG ELECTRIC HEAT

Assembly Code	Thermal Resistance of Illustrated Assembly (m² C°/W)	Required Thermal Resistance (NECH)	Components From Interior to Exterior
F2	1.52	1.30	• 100 mm concrete • Rigid insulation 33 mm XTPs board type IV
R1	10.53	9.00	• 13 mm gypsum board • Vapour barrier • 38 x 89 mm wood trusses @ 610 mm O.C. • Insulation 425 mm loose-fill mineral cellulose • Ventilated attic space
W1	4.18	4.10	• 13 mm gypsum board • Vapour barrier • 38 x 140 mm wood studs 406 mm O.C. • Insulation 140 mm high-density mineral fibre batts • Sheathing 25 mm XTPS board • Sheathing paper • Vinyl or aluminum siding
W2	5.11	4.10	• 13 mm gypsum board • Vapour barrier • 38 x 140 mm wood studs @ 406 mm O.C. • Insulation 140 mm sprayed polyurethane foam • 25 mm extruded polystyrene • 200 mm concrete
W3	3.40	3.10	• 13 mm gypsum board • Vapour barrier • 38 x 89 mm wood studs @ 406 mm O.C. • Insulation 89 mm high-density mineral fibre batts • Sheathing 38 mm expanded polystyrene
Window	Energy Rating of Window	Required Energy Rating (operable windows)	Window Description (all windows operable or with sash)
	-1	-6	• Triple glazing • 12.7 mm air-gap • Low-e • Foam-filled vinyl or fibreglass

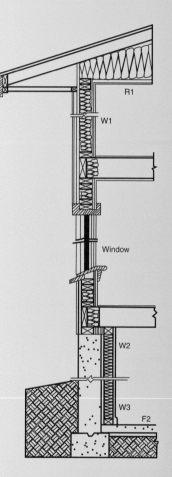

OTTAWA GAS HEAT

Assembly Code	Thermal Resistance of Illustrated Assembly (m² C°/W)	Required Thermal Resistance (NECH)	Components From Interior to Exterior
F2	1.99	1.60	• 100 mm concrete • Insulation 51 mm extruded polystyrene
R1	7.13	5.80	• 13 mm gypsum board • Vapour barrier • 38 x 89 mm wood trusses @ 610 mm O.C. • Insulation 265 mm medium-density mineral fibre batts • Ventilated attic space
W1	3.05	2.90	• 13 mm gypsum board • Vapour barrier • 38 x 140 mm wood Studs @ 406 mm O.C. • Insulation 140 mm low-density mineral fibre batts • 11 mm fibreboard sheathing • Sheathing paper • Vinyl or aluminum siding
W2	3.04	2.90	• 13 mm gypsum board • Vapour barrier • 38 x 89 mm wood studs @ 406 mm O.C. • Insulation 89 mm medium-density mineral fibre batts • 29 mm semi-rigid glass fibre • 200 mm concrete
W3	1.95	1.90	• 13 mm gypsum board • Vapour barrier • 38 x 89 mm wood studs @ 406 mm O.C. • Insulation 89 mm low-density mineral fibre batts • 200 mm concrete
Window	Energy Rating of Window	Required Energy Rating (operable windows)	Window Description (all windows operable or with sash)
	-12	-13	• Double glazing • 12.7 mm argon-fill • Low-e • Wood frame

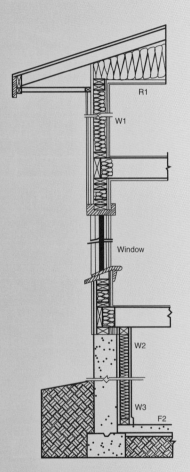

R1
W1
Window
W2
W3
F2

OTTAWA ELECTRIC HEAT

Assembly Code	Thermal Resistance of Illustrated Assembly (m² C°/W)	Required Thermal Resistance (NECH)	Components From Interior to Exterior
F2	1.99	1.60	• 100 mm concrete • Insulation 51 mm extruded polystyrene
R1	10.53	9.00	• 13 mm gypsum board • Vapour barrier • 38 x 89 mm wood trusses @ 610 mm O.C. • Insulation 425 mm loose-fill mineral cellulose • Ventilated attic space
W1	4.47	4.40	• 13 mm gypsum board • Vapour barrier • 38 x 140 mm wood studs @ 406 mm O.C. • Insulation 140 mm high-density mineral fibre batts • Sheathing 38 mm semi-rigid glass fibre • Sheathing paper • Vinyl or aluminum siding
W2	5.11	4.40	• 13 mm gypsum board • Vapour barrier • 38 x 140 mm wood studs @ 406 mm O.C. • Insulation 140 mm sprayed polyurethane foam • 25 mm extruded polystyrene • 200 mm concrete
W3	3.23	3.10	• 13 mm gypsum board • Vapour barrier • 38 x 89 mm wood studs @ 406 mm O.C. • Insulation 89 mm high-density mineral fibre batts • 31 mm extruded polystyrene • 200 mm concrete
Window	Energy Rating of Window	Required Energy Rating (operable windows)	Window Description (all windows operable or with sash)
	-10	-10	• Double glazing • 12.7 mm argon-Fill • Low-e • Vinyl frame

Design	Orientation of Front of House	Floor Area (excluding unfinished basement) (m²)	South Glass to Floor Area (%)	Individual Space Heating Ottawa Envelope for Gas Heat		Solar Fraction
				kW h	KW h/m²	
Detached						
1	S	137	5.6	15,760	115	0.24
2	N	150	5.2	16,050	107	0.21
3	N	139	11.4	13,070	94	0.38
4	N	204	6.5	21,630	106	0.27
5	SW	234	6.6	18,250	78	0.30
6	N	186	6.4	21,820	117	0.22
7	N	256	6.3	24,830	97	0.28
8	N	142	13.0	14,2000	100	0.39
9	S	142	10.4	14,490	102	0.36
Average (Detached)				17,850	102	0.29
Semidetached						
10	N	121	6.8	12,220	101	0.28
11	S	129	5.7	13,930	108	0.27
12	S	142	2.9	13,210	93	0.18
13	N	122	8.8	12,310	101	0.33
14	N	154	8.4	14,480	94	0.34
Average (Semidetached)				13,230	99	0.28
Townhouses						
15	S	134	3.5	9,250	69	0.22
16	S	116	6.2	11,020	95	0.38
17	N	119	5.3	9,640	81	0.22
18	N	104	6.1	8,010	77	0.29
19	S	110	5.3	7,150	65	0.29
20	S	118	8.4	8,030	68	0.35
Average (Townhouses)				8,850	76	0.29

Table 3.2 Summary performance of designs

Note:
Column 4 is south-glass area, not window area

Design 1

This two-storey house is designed for the north side of an east-west street, so that the street side of the house faces south. The design provides a total floor area of 137 m² and a basement. The original design location is Toronto.

Solar Features

The house has been designed with most of the window area located on the south side facing the street. Little glass area has been provided on the other sides of the house, but natural light is provided to virtually every room. The total glass-to-floor-area ratio is 9.9 percent. The southern glass-to-floor-area ratio is 5.6 percent.

The most striking solar feature of this traditionally elegant design is the large two-storey sunspace entry. This space connects the ground floor, front hall and stairwell with the second floor.

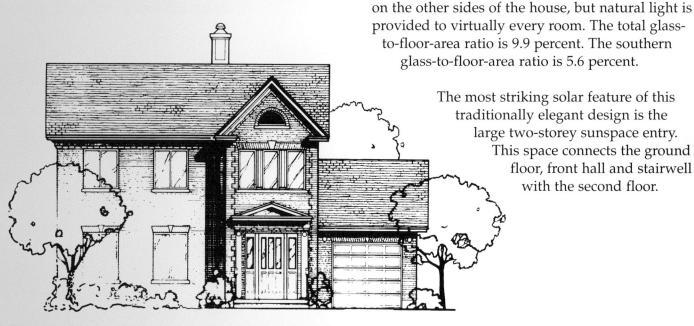

View from the street (south side of house)

On the ground floor, a sunny living room includes a decorative masonry alcove and wood stove. The U-shaped kitchen has a convenient full-wall pantry and is connected to a breakfast nook and dining room. The dining room opens onto a rear deck through patio doors.

Upstairs, the design includes a large master bedroom with a three-piece ensuite bathroom and a walk-in closet with dressing area. Two additional bedrooms, the main bathroom and an open landing complete the second storey.

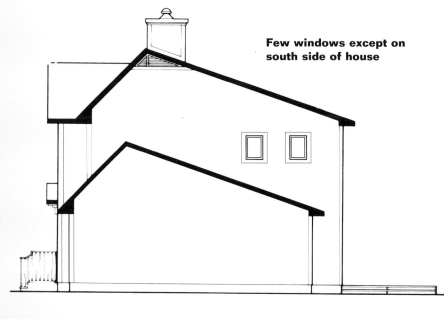

Few windows except on south side of house

East side of house

House has compact shape to maximize energy efficiency

SECOND FLOOR

Landing overlooks two-storey sunspace, providing views to the ground-floor entry area and to the outside

High-level return air inlet above sunspace assists circulation of passive solar gain

Window area is concentrated on the south side of the house

The upper gallery is provided with a high air-return grille for the forced-air heating system to recirculate passive solar gain (and heat from the wood stove). The compact shape of the house simplifies the circulation of solar gain and helps make the house energy efficient.

The asymmetrical roof design provides the correct slope for possible future active solar heating or photovoltaic cells while limiting roof height to minimize shading on adjacent properties.

Location	Design For	Annual Heating (kW h/m²)	Solar Fraction
Vancouver	Gas Heat	72	0.38
	Electric Heat	46	0.43
Ottawa	Gas Heat	115	0.24
	Electric Heat	71	0.32
Winnipeg	Gas Heat	138	0.18
	Electric Heat	122	0.20

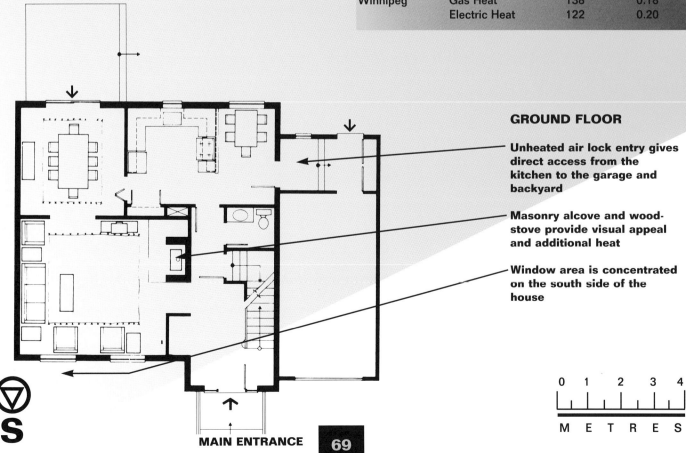

GROUND FLOOR

Unheated air lock entry gives direct access from the kitchen to the garage and backyard

Masonry alcove and wood-stove provide visual appeal and additional heat

Window area is concentrated on the south side of the house

S

MAIN ENTRANCE

0 1 2 3 4

M E T R E S

Design 2

This two-storey house is designed for the south side of an east-west street, so that the rear of the house faces south. The design requires an 18-m-wide lot to accommodate the single-car garage at the side.

Solar Features

This house has been designed with most of the windows on the south side. The windows on the north have been kept as small as possible while still recognizing the need for adequate light and the desirability of an attractive exterior appearance on the street side. There are only two windows on the east side and none on the west. The total glass-to-floor-area ratio is 9 percent. The southerly glass-to-floor-area ratio is 5.2 percent.

**Rear view
(south side of house)**

Roof slope of 45° permits future collection of solar energy through photovoltaic cells or solar collectors for hot water

Two-storey glass provides sunlight and solar gain to large two-storey space behind

The house has a floor area of about 150 m² on two levels plus a basement. The design features a centre-hall plan with a partially open staircase rising in the centre of the home. The ground floor offers a large kitchen connected to the dining room and a breakfast nook. The house also features a main-floor family room, which connects to both the breakfast nook and the living room. Upstairs, the design includes a master bedroom, two other bedrooms and a den that can serve as a fourth bedroom.

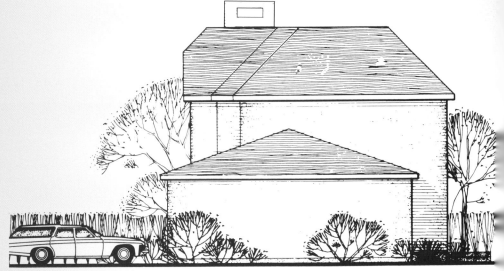

West side of house

Deciduous trees for summer shading

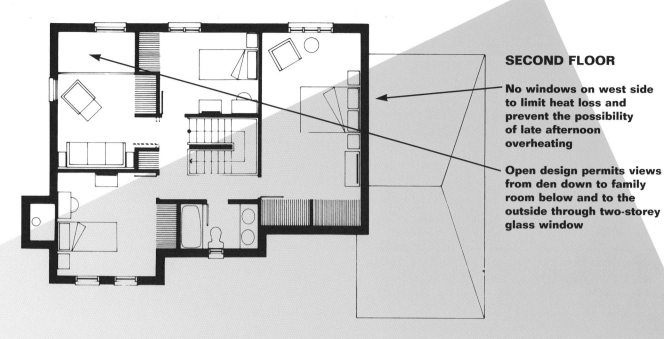

SECOND FLOOR

No windows on west side to limit heat loss and prevent the possibility of late afternoon overheating

Open design permits views from den down to family room below and to the outside through two-storey glass window

The most striking architectural feature of the home is the tall, south-facing glass window. The space directly behind the window rises two levels promoting natural ventilation.

The roof design features a 45° slope deliberately designed to permit the installation of a solar collector for hot water or photovoltaic cells at a future date. The recommended landscaping includes deciduous trees to control summer heat gain while minimizing loss of winter gain.

Location	Design For	Annual Heating (kW h/m²)	Solar Fraction
Vancouver	Gas Heat	66	0.33
	Electric Heat	45	0.38
Ottawa	Gas Heat	107	0.21
	Electric Heat	68	0.28
Winnipeg	Gas Heat	133	0.15
	Electric Heat	117	0.17

GROUND FLOOR

Two-storey space connects family room to den above

Bay windows are provided to add interest to both interior and exterior of house

S

MAIN ENTRANCE

0 1 2 3 4

M E T R E S

Design 3

This two-storey house is designed to be located on the south side of an east-west street, so that the rear of the house faces south. Although the long side of the house is oriented towards the south, the design is compact enough to allow construction on a lot only 15 m wide.

South side of house

The design provides a floor area of 139 m² plus a basement. The ground floor features a sunny living room with bay windows and a fireplace. The kitchen is large enough to provide a breakfast area. It is also bright because of the large window and patio doors opening onto a rear deck. A dining room, family room and powder room are also located on the ground floor.

The second floor features a master bedroom with ensuite bath, two additional bedrooms and the main bathroom. The stairway between floors is open, so that the short hallway on the second floor overlooks the front entry.

Solar Features

The design provides over 15 m² of glazing on the south face. The total glass-to-floor-area ratio is 14.8 percent; the south facade glass-to-floor-area ratio is 11.4 percent. (Because of the bay window, the actual percentage of south-facing glass would be lower). By placing hallways, stairways and utility areas on the north side, the design ensures that all main rooms receive direct solar gain except for the dining room and one second-floor bedroom

Additional thermal mass, provided by brick facing on the east and north walls in the living room (including the fireplace) and on the west and south walls in the family room, contributes to the high Solar Fraction and avoidance of overheating. Additional mass is provided in the south-facing rooms by double-thickness drywall on the ceiling and remaining walls.

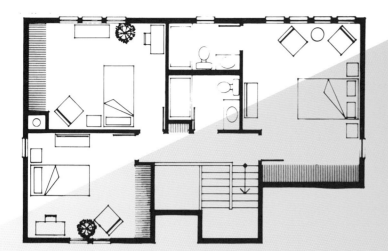

SECOND FLOOR

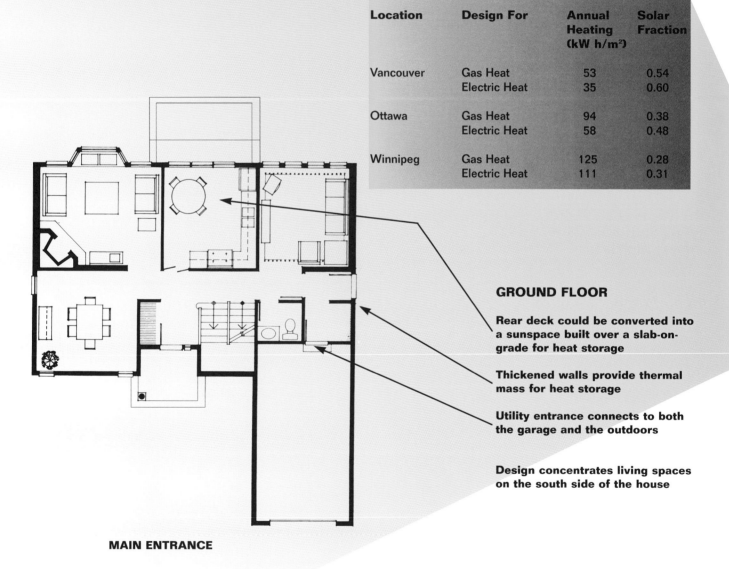

Location	Design For	Annual Heating (kW h/m²)	Solar Fraction
Vancouver	Gas Heat	53	0.54
	Electric Heat	35	0.60
Ottawa	Gas Heat	94	0.38
	Electric Heat	58	0.48
Winnipeg	Gas Heat	125	0.28
	Electric Heat	111	0.31

GROUND FLOOR

Rear deck could be converted into a sunspace built over a slab-on-grade for heat storage

Thickened walls provide thermal mass for heat storage

Utility entrance connects to both the garage and the outdoors

Design concentrates living spaces on the south side of the house

MAIN ENTRANCE

S

0 1 2 3 4

M E T R E S

Design 4

This two-storey, single-family home is designed for the south side of an east-west street, so that the rear of the house faces south. The design, which provides 203 m² of living space plus a basement, was prepared as part of the Advanced House Program and built in the Ottawa-Carleton area.

breakfast area improves the flow of sunshine during the early part of the day. An open-plan ground floor and open staircase enhance the home's natural air circulation. Roof overhangs are exaggerated to provide summer shade for the south-facing windows.

Manufactured shingles made from recycled sawdust imitate cedar shakes

Veranda gives the home a traditional look

View from the street

A centrally located kitchen provides easy access to adjacent breakfast, dining and family rooms. The family room, which opens onto the rear deck, has a gas fireplace. A separate living room, powder room, utility room and entry air lock are also on the ground floor. The upper level features a large master bedroom with ensuite bathroom and walk-in closet. Three other bedrooms and a second bathroom complete the second floor.

Solar Features

The house has been designed with most of its windows on the south, facing onto the rear garden. The north elevation is conservatively glazed, whereas the east-west glazing is minimal. The total glass-to-floor-area ratio is 11 percent; the south glass-to-floor-area ratio is 6.5 percent. The principal activity areas of the house are located on the south side, and a bay window for the

Photovoltaic panels on the original design could be replaced by solar water-heating panels

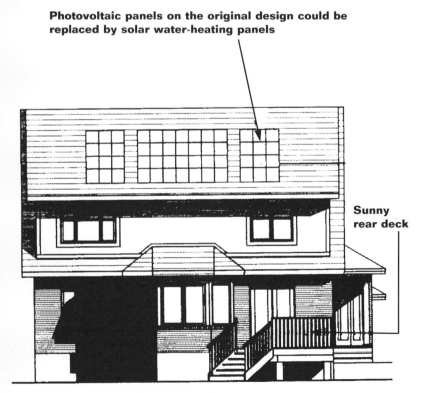

Sunny rear deck

South side of the house

74

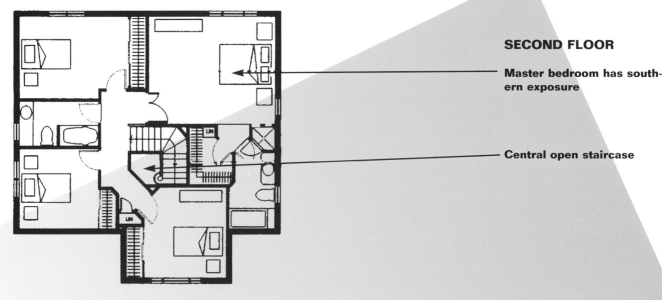

SECOND FLOOR

Master bedroom has south-ern exposure

Central open staircase

Advanced Features

The house uses a compact form, high insulation values (RSI 6.6 walls; RSI 10.6 ceiling) and airtight construction techniques to minimize heat loss. The windows are triple-glazed casement type with two low-emissivity coatings, krypton gas-fill and warm edge spacers (ER = 12 for fixed windows; -1 for operable windows). A direct-vented, high-efficiency, condensing gas-fired water heater provides both domestic hot water and space heating. Air distribution relies on an air handler in which the blower uses a high-efficiency electronically commutated motor.

Because of the low heat demand, 50 mm ducts were all that was required to deliver air to the rooms. Diffusers are centrally located (i.e., not below windows), minimizing duct runs and friction losses. A prefabricated and insulated duct work system limits duct heat and air loss, while an air-to-air heat exchanger and electronic air filter ensure good indoor air quality. A photovoltaic system using roof-mounted panels is also provided.

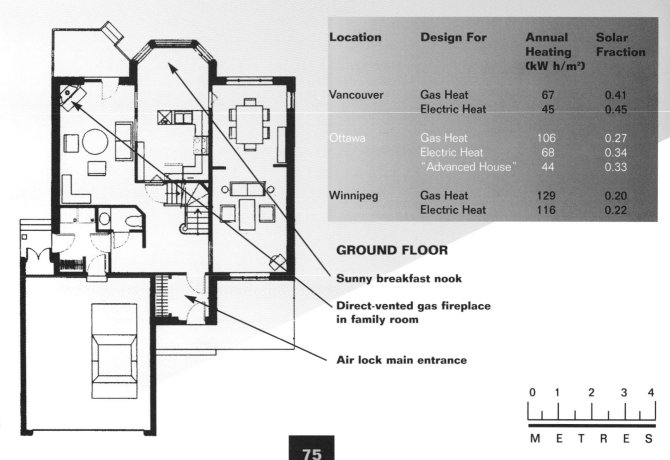

Location	Design For	Annual Heating (kW h/m²)	Solar Fraction
Vancouver	Gas Heat	67	0.41
	Electric Heat	45	0.45
Ottawa	Gas Heat	106	0.27
	Electric Heat	68	0.34
	"Advanced House"	44	0.33
Winnipeg	Gas Heat	129	0.20
	Electric Heat	116	0.22

GROUND FLOOR

Sunny breakfast nook

Direct-vented gas fireplace in family room

Air lock main entrance

S

0 1 2 3 4

M E T R E S

Design 5

This single-family home is designed for the northeast side of a northeast-southwest street, with garden areas located on the southeast and northeast sides of the dwelling. The home has 234 m² of living space on two levels. This innovative design, which was prepared as part of the

Steel roofing provides long life

Siding is made from recycled scrap wood

Verandah shades the southwest-facing glass

View from the street

Advanced House Program and built in Waterloo, Ontario, fully uses the basement for living space.

The floor layouts are non-traditional, with bedrooms and daytime activity areas mixed on the same level. The basement includes two bedrooms and a full bathroom, as well as a family room and office or study area. The master bedroom is located on the upper level along with a living area, kitchen, dining room and bathroom. The garage is oversized to make up for lack of storage space that would otherwise be found in an unfinished basement.

Solar Features

The house is designed with most of the windows on the southeast side. There is no northwest-facing window and northeast and southwest windows are limited. With appropriate grading, even the lower basement level receives adequate daylighting, while

the basement floor provides useful thermal mass. The total glass-to-floor-area ratio is 9.4 percent; the south glass-to-floor-area ratio is 6.6 percent. A dormer located at a high level allows natural light to penetrate to the back of the house. An interior vision-obscuring glass wall made from recycled glass admits natural light into the windowless bathroom on the north side.

Advanced Features

The house uses a compact form, high insulation levels (RSI 5.9 walls; RSI 10.6 ceiling) and airtight construction techniques to minimize heat losses. The windows are triple glazed with two low-emissivity coatings, argon gas-fill and insulated spacers. (ER values are 11 for fixed windows; 4 for operable windows.)

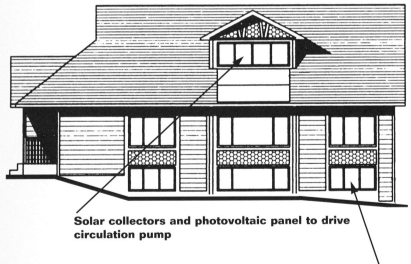

Solar collectors and photovoltaic panel to drive circulation pump

Lower "basement" level is fully utilized as living space

Southeast elevation

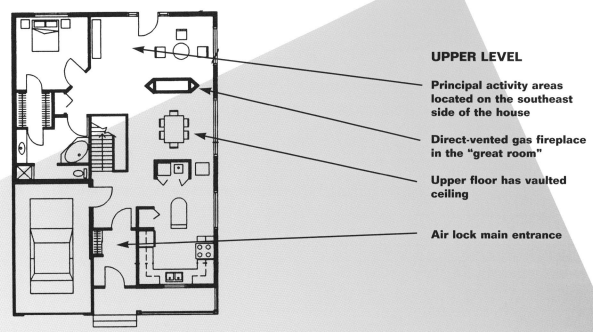

UPPER LEVEL

Principal activity areas located on the southeast side of the house

Direct-vented gas fireplace in the "great room"

Upper floor has vaulted ceiling

Air lock main entrance

The window frames are foam-insulated fibreglass. To reduce summer heat gains, some windows have thermochromic films that turn opaque above 24°C. Space heating and ventilation is handled by a prototype combined gas furnace and heat-recovery ventilator, using a rock bed to extract heat from the furnace flue gases. The ducts are oversized, and the bends provided with turning vanes to reduce friction losses. High-efficiency motors and pleated, as opposed to electrostatic, air filters further reduce air distribution energy loss. A prototype drywall containing recycled material provides additional thermal mass as compared to traditional (22.5 mm) gypsum drywall board.

Location	Design For	Annual Heating (kW h/m²)	Solar Fraction
Vancouver	Gas Heat	61	0.40
	Electric Heat	33	0.50
Ottawa	Gas Heat	78	0.30
	Electric Heat	50	0.39
	"Advanced House"	41	0.35
Winnipeg	Gas Heat	99	0.22
	Electric Heat	92	0.24

LOWER LEVEL

Area could be partitioned to create quiet study, office or fourth bedroom

Bedrooms in basement provide cooler more comfortable sleeping contitions winter and summer

S

0 1 2 3 4

METRES

Design 6

This two-storey, single-family home is designed for the south side of an east-west street, so that the rear of the house faces south. The design, which provides 186 m² of living space plus a basement, was prepared as part of the Advanced House

Long-life pine roof shakes

View from the street

Program and built in Winnipeg, Manitoba. Conventional in appearance, this home features an open-plan kitchen, dinette and family room on the south side of the dwelling, with the dining or living room, bathroom and a fourth bedroom to the north. A master bedroom with ensuite bathroom, two other bedrooms and a shared bathroom are on the upper level. A large deck is provided off the south side of the house. It is accessible from the kitchen and dinette.

Solar Features

Glazing is concentrated on the south, and the glass area is limited on all other elevations. The glazing on the ground floor of the west wall has been angled at 45° to face the southwest for higher gains and

to avoid the adverse effects of west glazing. The total glass-to-floor-area ratio is 10.5 percent; the south glass-to-floor-area ratio is 6.4 percent. Removable screens are provided to prevent over-heating in summer, and the south-facing glazing on the ground floor is shaded by the master bedroom balcony above. An open-plan layout on the ground floor promotes air circulation. Two of the bathrooms avoid condensation problems by eliminating windows.

Advanced Features

A compact floor plan, high insulation values (RSI 7.9 walls; RSI 10.5 ceiling) and airtight construction practices minimize heat losses. Windows are quadruple glazed with three low-emissivity films, krypton gas-fill and insulated

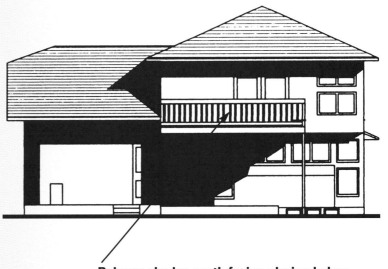

Balcony shades south-facing glazing below

South side of the house

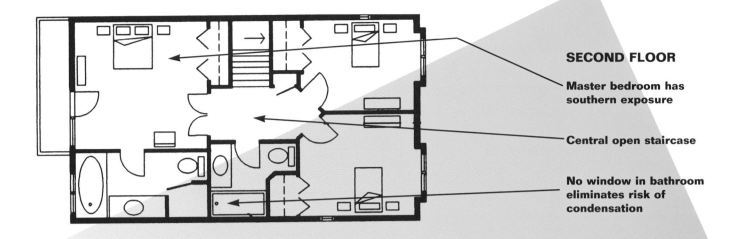

SECOND FLOOR

Master bedroom has southern exposure

Central open staircase

No window in bathroom eliminates risk of condensation

spacers (with ER values of 7 for fixed windows and -7 for operable windows.) A direct-vented, high-efficiency condensing gas-fired water heater provides both domestic hot water and space heating. Air circulation fan motors are the high-efficiency type. The air-circulation system is zoned, and separate thermostats allow individual temperature control in four separate areas. To reduce heat loss around the basement, a heat-recovery ventilator is provided, and warm air is drawn from the attic through basement drainage tiles.

Location	Design For	Annual Heating (kW h/m²)	Solar Fraction
Vancouver	Gas Heat	76	0.35
	Electric Heat	51	0.40
Ottawa	Gas Heat	117	0.22
	Electric Heat	75	0.29
Winnipeg	Gas Heat	141	0.16
	Electric Heat	126	0.18
	"Advanced House"	79	0.26

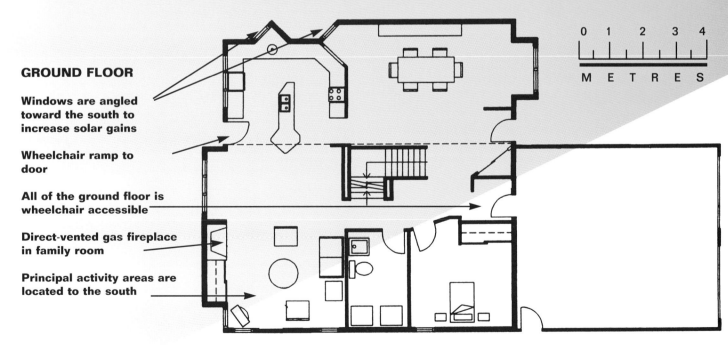

GROUND FLOOR

Windows are angled toward the south to increase solar gains

Wheelchair ramp to door

All of the ground floor is wheelchair accessible

Direct-vented gas fireplace in family room

Principal activity areas are located to the south

Design 7

This two-storey, single-family home built over an unheated crawl space is designed for the south side of an east-west street, so that the rear of the house faces south. The design, which provides 256 m² of living space plus a garage, was built in a Vancouver suburb.

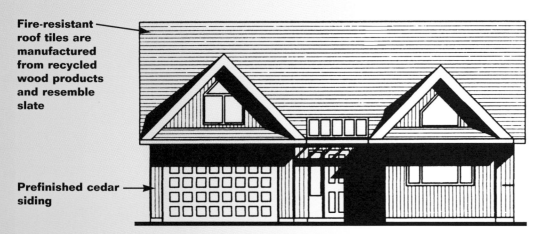

Fire-resistant roof tiles are manufactured from recycled wood products and resemble slate

Prefinished cedar siding

View from the street

A ground floor "great room" adjoins the dining room and kitchen on the south side of the home. A master bedroom with ensuite bathroom and walk-in closet takes up the west side, with the media room and garage on the north and east. The upper level offers three additional bedrooms, two full bathrooms, a small library and storage rooms. The central staircase is open between floors, as is the vaulted roof above the great room and the media room.

Solar Features

This home uses large windows to provide an abundance of natural light throughout. Glazing is predominant on the south elevation. The total glass-to-floor-area ratio is 10.8 percent; the south glass-to-floor-area ratio is 6.3 percent. An open-plan layout on the ground floor promotes air circulation, as do the vaulted ceilings and

two-storey spaces. A return-air grille located at a high level on the upper floor returns solar heated warm air to the heating system air handler.

Advanced Features

A relatively compact floor plan, high insulation values (RSI 5.45 walls; RSI 7.74 ceiling) and airtight construction practices minimize heat losses. Windows are casement and wood-framed triple-glaze with two low-emissivity layers, gas-fill and insulated spacers. (ER values are -5 for fixed and operable windows.) A direct-vented, high-efficiency condensing gas-fired water heater provides both domestic hot water and

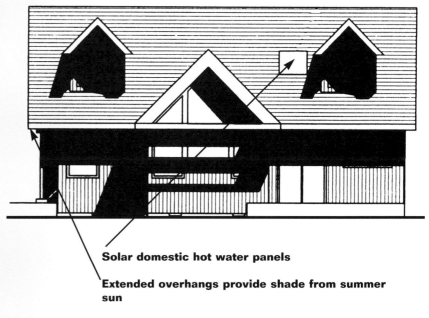

Solar domestic hot water panels

Extended overhangs provide shade from summer sun

Deciduous trees planned for the west side provide summer shade while avoiding loss of winter solar gains

South side of the house

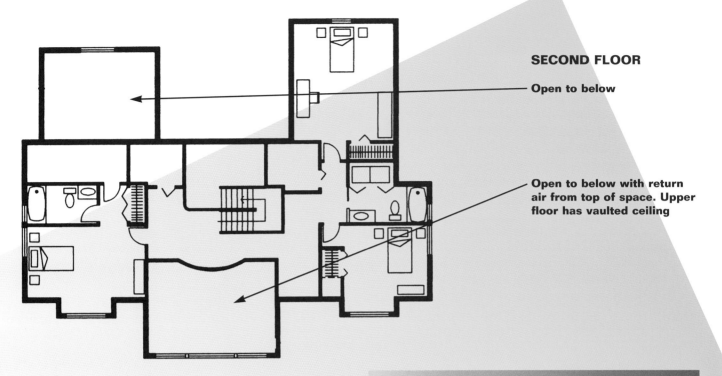

SECOND FLOOR

Open to below

Open to below with return air from top of space. Upper floor has vaulted ceiling

space heating. Solar collectors on the roof preheat domestic hot water, and a solar cell provides power for the pump. A zoned air-distribution system allows individual temperature control for four different areas. The air-handler blower uses a high-efficiency motor. A heat-recovery ventilator and bag-type filter ensure good indoor air quality. A ducted outdoor air intake allows the air handler to be used for "free-cooling" in summer. A home-automation system is also included.

Location	Design For	Annual Heating (kW h/m²)	Solar Fraction
Vancouver	Gas Heat	78	0.38
	Electric Heat	57	0.43
	"Advanded House"	22	0.51
Ottawa	Gas Heat	97	0.28
	Electric Heat	69	0.34
Winnipeg	Gas Heat	129	0.19
	Electric Heat	120	0.20

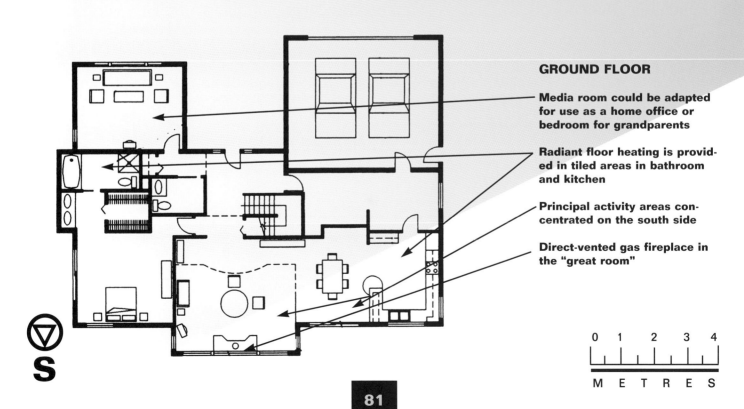

GROUND FLOOR

Media room could be adapted for use as a home office or bedroom for grandparents

Radiant floor heating is provided in tiled areas in bathroom and kitchen

Principal activity areas concentrated on the south side

Direct-vented gas fireplace in the "great room"

S

0 1 2 3 4

M E T R E S

Design 8

This two-storey house is designed to be located on the south side of an east-west street, so that the rear of the house faces south. The unit fits on a 15-m-wide lot, but an even wider lot would be better because the design features a deck at the side of the house. The house provides 142 m² of living space plus a basement.

Solar Features

The design provides about 19 m² of south-facing glass area but very little glass area on the other sides of the house. The total glass-to-floor-area ratio is 15 percent; the south glass-to-floor-area ratio is 13 percent. To prevent overheating, mass has been provided in the form of brick facing surrounding the fireplace and on the north wall in the kitchen-family room combination. All other wall and ceiling surfaces in the south part of the house have 25-mm-thick drywall.

Rear view (south side of house)

Large glass area opens onto two-storey sunspace

On the ground floor, the dining and living rooms are connected in an open plan focussing on a free-standing central fireplace. Access to the outside deck is from the living room. The dining room is open above, providing a striking two-storey space. The kitchen and family room are part of a single open space, separated by a bar-style breakfast area and a step-down into the sunken family room.

On the upper level, the hallway and one of the bedrooms overlook the dining room, providing a view into the two-storey space. The main bedroom, the master bedroom with ensuite bath and walk-in closet, and a third bedroom are also located on the second floor.

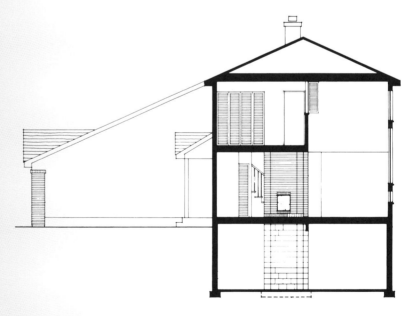

Section of house (looking from the west)

Second-storey bedroom overlooks two-storey sunspace. The open exposure from the bedroom can be closed off with shutters for privacy

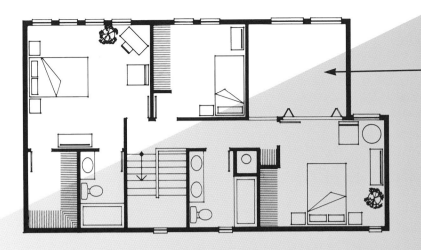

SECOND FLOOR

Open area above dining room provides striking two-storey space that also provides for natural circulation of air

The single most striking feature in this home is the two-storey sunspace above the dining room. It provides a large part of the solar gain and allows for natural circulation of the heat. The shallow depth of the house, the open layout and the careful positioning of living areas to the south ensure that all of the main rooms receive solar gain. The design calls for a forced-air heating system to distribute heat and prevent overheating.

Location	Design For	Annual Heating (kW h/m²)	Solar Fraction
Vancouver	Gas Heat	58	0.55
	Electric Heat	38	0.62
Ottawa	Gas Heat	100	0.39
	Electric Heat	61	0.49
Winnipeg	Gas Heat	131	0.29
	Electric Heat	117	0.32

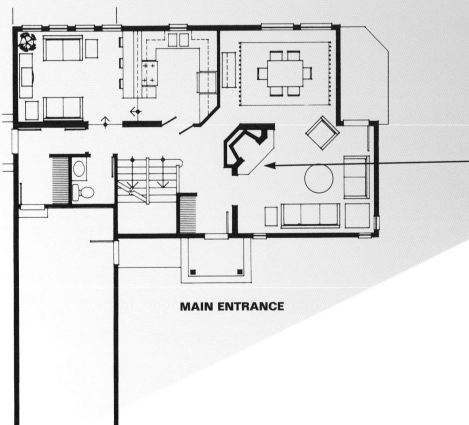

GROUND FLOOR

The fireplace is a focal point of the living and dining areas. The face brick surrounding it provides important thermal storage

MAIN ENTRANCE

S

0 1 2 3 4

METRES

Design 9

ABOUT THIS DESIGN

This two-storey house is designed for the north side of an east-west street, so that the street side of the house faces south. The lot should be 15 m wide, and the house provides 142 m² of floor area plus a basement.

View from street (south side)

The design features a modified centre-hall concept with utility areas at the rear of the house (the north side) and living areas at the front. The most striking feature of the house is a two-storey open space above the living room. Because this space is centrally located at the second-floor level, it opens onto the central hall, the master bedroom and a second bedroom. Thus, most areas on the second floor have a pleasing view into the living room and to the outside.

On the ground floor, the dining room is also positioned against the south wall. On the north side are the kitchen and a small breakfast area, with patio doors opening onto a rear deck. The staircase and powder room are also located at the rear, adjacent to an entrance from the garage.

Solar Features

The south-facing wall of this house includes about 15 m² of glass area. The total glass-to-floor-area ratio is 16 percent; and the south glass-to-floor-area ratio is 10.4 percent. Extra thermal mass is provided to prevent overheating.

The most striking area of mass is found in the fireplace and chimney, which extends a full two stories through the open space above the living room. The mass is formed of 100-mm concrete blocks covered with a stucco-like interior finish. The same materials are also used on the west walls of the living room and on the north wall of the family

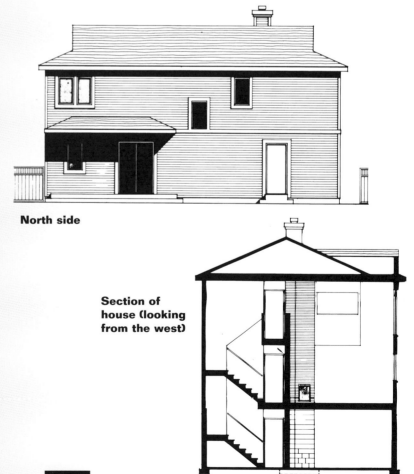

North side

Section of house (looking from the west)

84

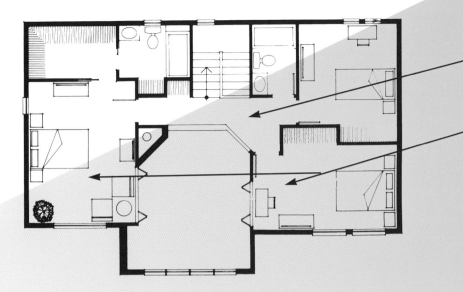

Upper hallway creates interesting bridge effect between atrium and stairwell

Bedrooms overlook atrium, with shutters to provide privacy when required

Some walls incorporate concrete block and stucco finish to provide additional thermal mass. Other walls in south area use double drywall

room. All remaining surfaces in the south part of the house have a double layer of drywall finish to provide additional mass.

The two-storey, atrium-like space opening onto three distinct areas on the second floor assists natural air circulation (particularly when the doors are left open), as does the open stairway at the rear. Fans or the forced-air heating system further improves heat distribution. During the summer, the south-facing window areas should be shaded with blinds or retractable canvas awnings to control potential overheating.

Location	Design For	Annual Heating (kW h/m²)	Solar Fraction
Vancouver	Gas Heat	61	0.52
	Electric Heat	40	0.58
Ottawa	Gas Heat	102	0.36
	Electric Heat	63	0.46
Winnipeg	Gas Heat	132	0.27
	Electric Heat	117	0.29

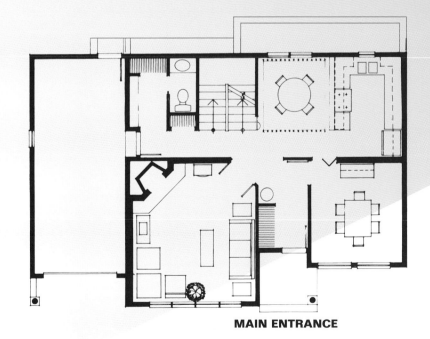

MAIN ENTRANCE

GROUND FLOOR

Garage is located beneath master bedroom

S

```
0   1   2   3   4
|_|_|_|_|_|_|_|_|
M E T R E S
```

Design 10

This two-storey, semidetached house is designed to be built on the south side of an east-west street, so that the rear of the house faces south. The dwelling is planned for a 25-m-wide lot (for both units). The garages are located at the front of the

Rear view (south side of house)

house. They have been turned parallel to the street to allow the house to be set reasonably close to the road and to make the best use of backyard space.

On the ground floor, each unit contains a living room with a fireplace and patio doors that open onto a rear deck. There is a separate dining room with easy connection to both the kitchen and the living room. The kitchen has sufficient space for a breakfast area. Upstairs, there are three bedrooms, one bathroom and a linen closet. In total, each of the two units provides 121 m² of space plus a basement.

This design lends itself to a variety of exterior treatments. Apart from changes to the roof pitch and type, or changes to the type of siding, consideration could be given to changing the layout of the garages. One garage could be turned to face the street and the other could run parallel to the street. A curved driveway would be required.

Solar Features

While the house is long and thin, resulting in higher heat losses than a more compact structure, the design allows direct solar gain to all of its major living areas. The total glass-to-floor-area ratio is 10.6 percent; and the south glass-to-floor-area ratio is 6.8 percent. If additional south-facing glass is desired, thermal mass could be introduced into the walls and floors in the living, dining and kitchen areas to limit overheating.

Party wall

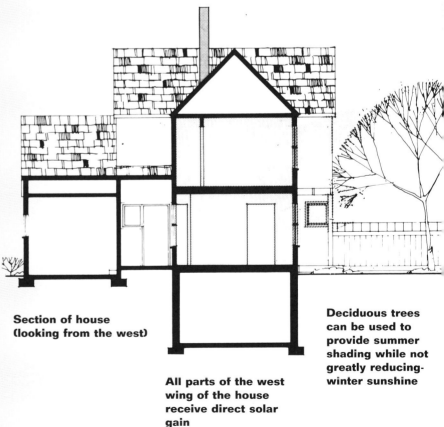

Section of house (looking from the west)

All parts of the west wing of the house receive direct solar gain

Deciduous trees can be used to provide summer shading while not greatly reducing winter sunshine

86

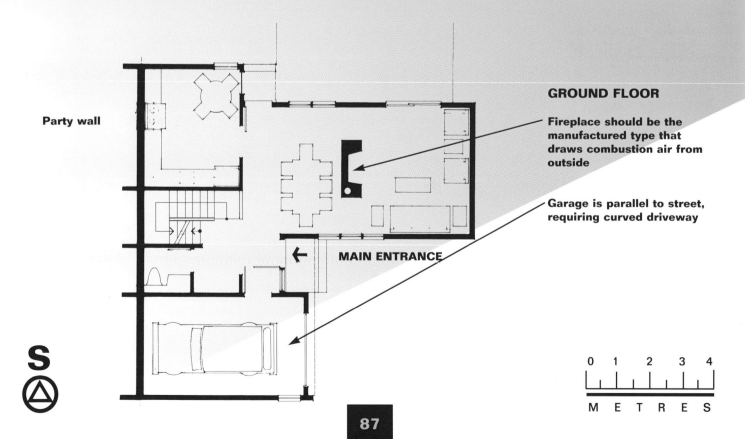

SECOND FLOOR

Fourth bedroom can be provided over the garage and connected to the rest of the upstairs by converting the linen closet into a corridor

Party wall

One possibility for increasing the south-facing glass area lends itself particularly to a sloped site (sloping away to the north). In such a case, larger windows could be added to the basement wall to provide solar gain and, with proper design and insulation, the basement floor could be used for storage. A similar option can be pursued on a flat site if the grade and the height of the foundation are adjusted.

Location	Design For	Annual Heating (kW h/m²)	Solar Fraction
Vancouver	Gas Heat	62	0.42
	Electric Heat	40	0.49
Ottawa	Gas Heat	101	0.28
	Electric Heat	63	0.36
Winnipeg	Gas Heat	127	0.21
	Electric Heat	114	0.23

GROUND FLOOR

Fireplace should be the manufactured type that draws combustion air from outside

Garage is parallel to street, requiring curved driveway

Party wall

← MAIN ENTRANCE

S

0 1 2 3 4

M E T R E S

Design 11

This two-storey, semidetached home is designed for the north side of an east-west street, so that the front of the house faces south. It has a conventional design with a square plan and a garage on the side. The cost of construction should be moderate.

Solar Features

On the ground floor, the garage takes up some of the southern exposure, but because the combined living-and-dining room extends the full depth of

Party wall

Overhanging bay window provides summer shading for living room window

View from street (south side)

The house provides 129 m² of living space plus a basement. The kitchen provides open and convenient access to the basement, allowing for possible future development.

The ground floor consists of a large L-shaped living-and-dining-room combination. French doors open off the living room onto a large sun deck at the front of the house. At the rear of the house, the kitchen-breakfast nook is located adjacent to the dining room, and a pass-through is provided between the kitchen and the dining room. A door from the breakfast nook gives access to the rear yard. There is also a pantry and a powder room.

On the upper level, there are three bedrooms and a single bathroom. The master bedroom has private access to the bathroom through a walk-in closet.

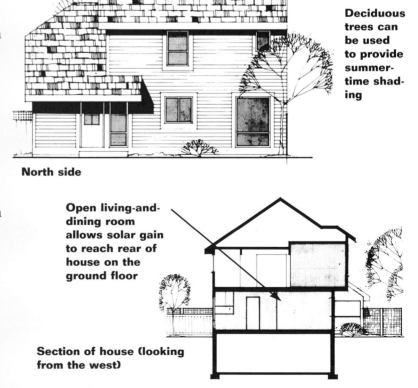

Party wall

Deciduous trees can be used to provide summertime shading

North side

Open living-and-dining room allows solar gain to reach rear of house on the ground floor

Section of house (looking from the west)

88

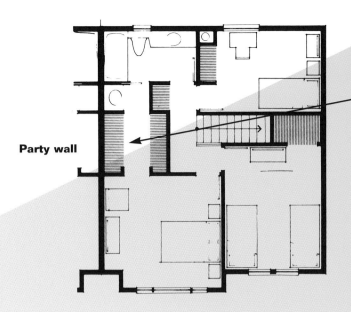

SECOND FLOOR

Walk-through closet provides direct access to bathroom and has an additional basin

Party wall

the house, a reasonable portion of the living area receives direct solar gain.

On the second floor, two of the three bedrooms receive direct solar gain. The large bay window in the master bedroom, apart from its visual interest, provides summer shading for the large window below. The total glass-to-floor-area ratio is 10.5 percent, and the south glass-to-floor-area ratio is 5.7 percent. Additional south-facing glass can be provided for greater solar contribution. However, the use of a circulating fan then becomes very important as natural air circulation is limited.

Location	Design For	Annual Heating (kW h/m²)	Solar Fraction
Vancouver	Gas Heat	69	0.41
	Electric Heat	42	0.48
Ottawa	Gas Heat	108	0.27
	Electric Heat	65	0.35
Winnipeg	Gas Heat	127	0.20
	Electric Heat	115	0.22

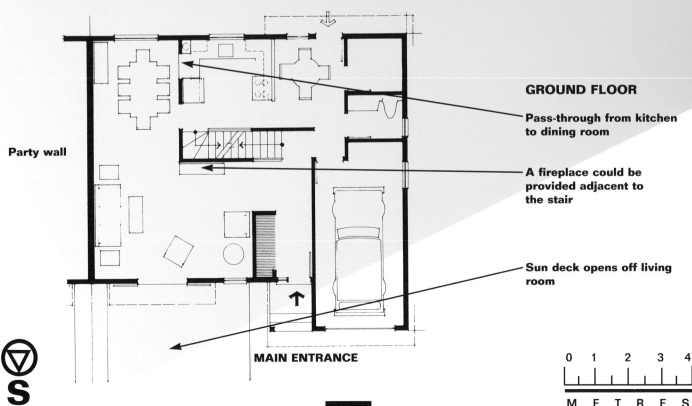

Party wall

S

MAIN ENTRANCE

GROUND FLOOR

Pass-through from kitchen to dining room

A fireplace could be provided adjacent to the stair

Sun deck opens off living room

```
0   1   2   3   4
M E T R E S
```

Design 12

This two-storey, semidetached house is designed to be built on the north side of an east-west street, so that the street side of the house faces south. Designed for a 22-m-wide lot, it provides 142 m² of floor space plus a basement. The design as presented does not include a garage.

Solar Features

The total glass-to-floor-area ratio is 5.4 percent; and the south glass-to-floor-area ratio is 2.9 percent. The party wall between the two units has high thermal mass that provides heat storage.

Both halves of semi-detached house are shown

View from street (south side)

On the ground floor, there is a spacious living room with a fireplace and a large south-facing window. The dining room at the rear opens onto the living room and has direct access to the kitchen, which is large enough to accommodate a breakfast area. On the second floor, there are three bedrooms and a main bathroom. The master bedroom features a large walk-in closet and a large south-facing window.

Two different options for the exterior of the house are presented. The first emphasizes the existence of two separate units within the double by repeating the same visual pattern on both sides (in mirror image). The other facade provides a unifying roof over the two units.

South side (alternative facade)

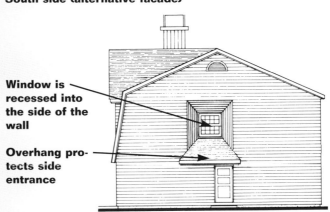

Window is recessed into the side of the wall

Overhang protects side entrance

East side of House

Roof detail would change slightly if the alternative facade for the south face of the house were used

Facade of house can be changed without changing interior design

90

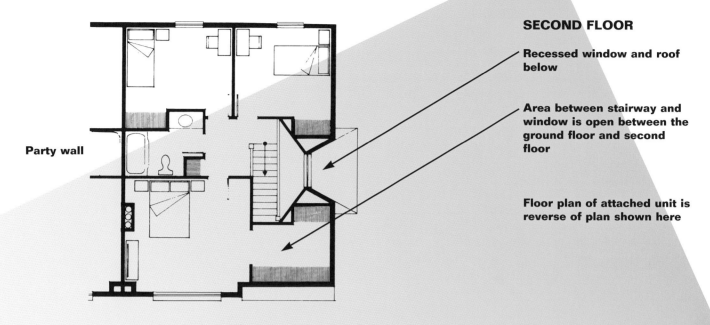

SECOND FLOOR

Recessed window and roof below

Area between stairway and window is open between the ground floor and second floor

Floor plan of attached unit is reverse of plan shown here

Party wall

A thermostatically controlled circulation fan that operates when the temperature in south-facing rooms rises above the set temperature distributes the solar gain.

Location	Design For	Annual Heating (kW h/m²)	Solar Fraction
Vancouver	Gas Heat	61	0.30
	Electric Heat	35	0.35
Ottawa	Gas Heat	93	0.18
	Electric Heat	55	0.25
Winnipeg	Gas Heat	105	0.13
	Electric Heat	94	0.15

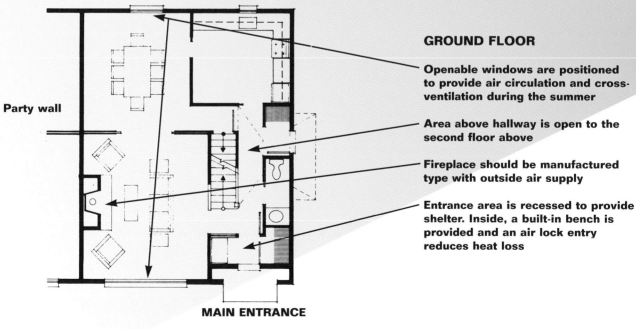

GROUND FLOOR

Openable windows are positioned to provide air circulation and cross-ventilation during the summer

Area above hallway is open to the second floor above

Fireplace should be manufactured type with outside air supply

Entrance area is recessed to provide shelter. Inside, a built-in bench is provided and an air lock entry reduces heat loss

Party wall

MAIN ENTRANCE

0 1 2 3 4

METRES

Design 13

This two-storey, semidetached unit is designed to be built on the south side of an east-west street, so that the rear of the house faces south. The house fits a narrow lot, such as an older infill lot commonly found close to the centre of established

Party wall

View from street (north side)

cities. At the front of the house, a courtyard and covered walkway lead to the front door. With careful landscaping and skylights in the roof of the walkway, an attractive entrance is presented to visitors. The interior of the house provides 122 (or 129) m² of floor space plus a basement.

On the ground floor, there is a living room with a fireplace and patio doors leading to a rear deck. The kitchen also has a door onto the rear deck and is large enough to include a small breakfast area. The dining room is adjacent to the kitchen and is built with a two-storey open space above it.

On the second floor, two of the bedrooms overlook the dining room, providing a pleasing view to the ground floor and the outside. The master bedroom, at the front of the house, includes a small dressing alcove and a door into the main bathroom (which also opens into the hall).

Solar Features

The total glass-to-floor-area ratio is 14.8 percent; and the south glass-to-floor-area ratio is 8.8 percent. On the main floor, all living areas are provided with south-facing windows, although the living room windows will be shaded in the morning (or in the afternoon on the other side of the building).

Party wall

Rear view (south side)

Strong gable ends and steeply pitched roof provide an exterior appearance more appropriate in an urban setting than a suburban subdivision

Deciduous trees can be used to provide summertime shading

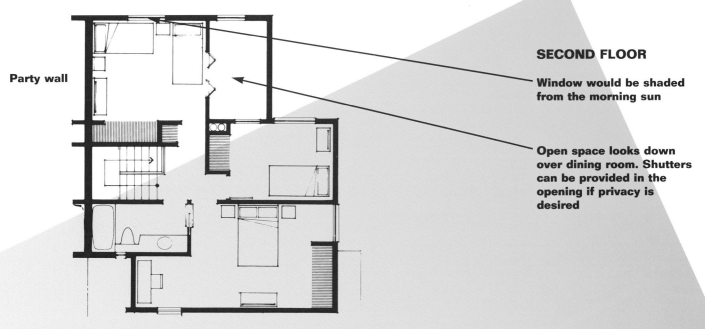

SECOND FLOOR

Window would be shaded from the morning sun

Open space looks down over dining room. Shutters can be provided in the opening if privacy is desired

Party wall

Upstairs, only the master bedroom does not receive direct sunlight, and one of the south-facing bedrooms will be shaded in the same way as the living room below. The open two-storey space above the dining room provides natural circulation of the solar gain, which could be enhanced by a two-speed fan installed on the forced-air furnace.

Location	Design For	Annual Heating (kW h/m²)	Solar Fraction
Vancouver	Gas Heat	62	0.48
	Electric Heat	40	0.33
Ottawa	Gas Heat	101	0.33
	Electric Heat	62	0.43
Winnipeg	Gas Heat	125	0.25
	Electric Heat	113	0.27

GROUND FLOOR

Design provides for enclosed courtyard in this area

Two-storey space above dining room provides striking visual appeal and circulation of solar gain

Fireplace should be manufactured type that uses exterior combustion air

Covered walkway leads to main entrance

Party wall

MAIN ENTRANCE

S

0 1 2 3 4

METRES

93

Design 14

This semidetached house is designed to be built on the south side of an east-west street, so that the rear of the house faces south. Each unit provides 154 m² of floor space in a two-storey split-level design. In addition, there is a partial basement and a crawl space. The house will fit on a lot as narrow as 20 m.

Solar Features

The total glass-to-floor-area ratio is 12.9 percent; and the south glass-to-floor-area ratio is 8.4 percent. Because of the open layout and the skylight, the design allows almost every room in the house direct solar access. The open design also provides

Party wall

View from street (north side)

The main entrance to the house is on the upper portion of the ground floor, which also contains the kitchen and dining areas. The lower level of the ground floor contains a living room, family room and powder room. The living room is open to the dining area on the upper level and separated only by a railing. Most of the dining area is located in an atrium that rises past the second floor to the roof, where there is a skylight.

On the second level, two of the rooms open onto the atrium. They can be provided with shutters for privacy as required. The stairway between the floors is open, providing views down into the living room from three sides above. The upper level of the second floor contains two bedrooms, while the lower level contains the master bedroom. Attached to the master bedroom is a den or parents' retreat.

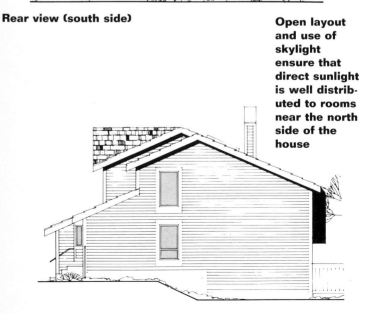

Party wall

Rear view (south side)

Open layout and use of skylight ensure that direct sunlight is well distributed to rooms near the north side of the house

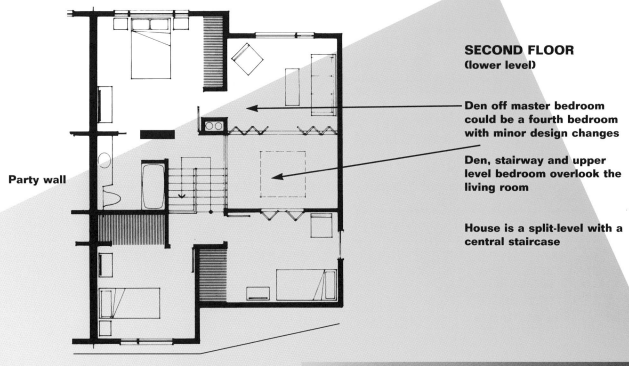

SECOND FLOOR
(lower level)

Den off master bedroom could be a fourth bedroom with minor design changes

Den, stairway and upper level bedroom overlook the living room

House is a split-level with a central staircase

Party wall

for good natural circulation of solar heat, which controls the temperature swing and creates a more comfortable indoor environment. The skylight is likely to create heat gain during the summer. It should be operable and fitted with blinds.

Location	Design For	Annual Heating (kW h/m²)	Solar Fraction
Vancouver	Gas Heat	61	0.45
	Electric Heat	38	0.55
Ottawa	Gas Heat	94	0.34
	Electric Heat	58	0.43
Winnipeg	Gas Heat	119	0.25
	Electric Heat	107	0.27

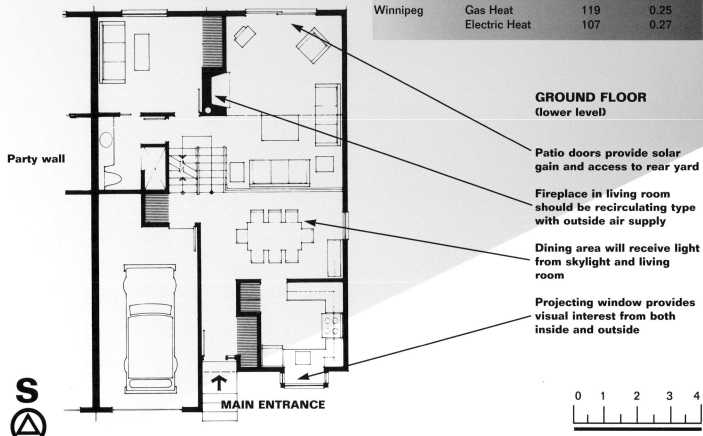

GROUND FLOOR
(lower level)

Party wall

Patio doors provide solar gain and access to rear yard

Fireplace in living room should be recirculating type with outside air supply

Dining area will receive light from skylight and living room

Projecting window provides visual interest from both inside and outside

S

MAIN ENTRANCE

0 1 2 3 4

M E T R E S

Design 15

This townhouse is designed to be built on the north side of an east-west street, so that the front of the house faces south. Each unit requires a 6-m-wide lot and has 134 m² of floor space and a basement.

Solar Features

The total glass-to-floor-area ratio is 5.2 percent; and the south glass-to-floor-area ratio is 3.5 percent. The relatively large size of the south-facing rooms means that a reasonable portion of the house receives direct solar gain. However, the depth of the house means that several rooms do not. Therefore, a fan is provided to draw solar heat from the south-facing rooms when temperatures rise above a preset level.

View from street (showing three units, south side)

The house is a split-level design with living space on two floors. The entry area, powder room and garage are located on a third, lower level. From the entry area, the stairs lead up to the lower half of the first floor, which contains the kitchen and dining area. A rear door off the kitchen opens onto the back deck. The upper half of the first floor features a spacious living room with a fireplace and direct access to a south-facing balcony. All three bedrooms and the main bathroom are on the second floor, split between the upper and lower levels.

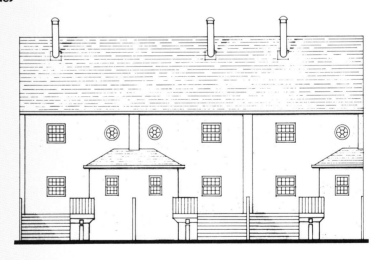

North side (showing three units)

Section of house (looking from the west)

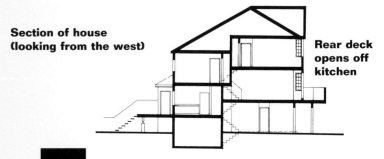

Rear deck opens off kitchen

SECOND FLOOR

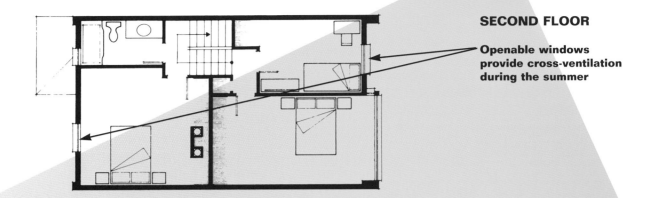

Openable windows provide cross-ventilation during the summer

The design allows the heat to be circulated to the basement, where the mass in the concrete floor provides additional heat storage. Further storage is provided by the concrete walls between each townhouse unit.

Location	Design For	Annual Heating (kW h/m²)	Solar Fraction
Vancouver	Gas Heat	39	0.33
	Electric Heat	24	0.43
Ottawa	Gas Heat	69	0.22
	Electric Heat	39	0.32
Winnipeg	Gas Heat	75	0.16
	Electric Heat	68	0.18

FIRST FLOOR

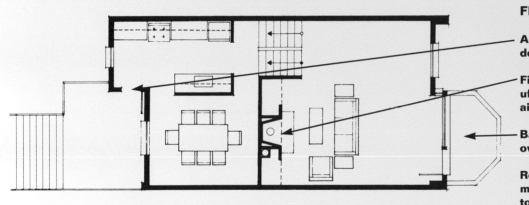

Access to rear door and deck via the kitchen area

Fireplace should be premanufactured type with outside air supply

Balcony off living room overlooks street

Room size is maximized by minimizing area given over to hallways

BASEMENT

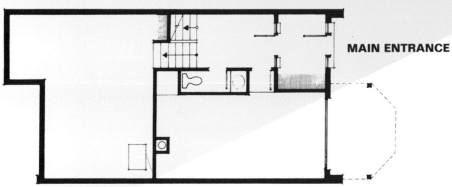

MAIN ENTRANCE

Front entrance includes an air lock entry to reduce heat loss

Note: Floor plan shown is for a single unit only. East and west walls are party walls shared with adjacent units

0 1 2 3 4

M E T R E S

Design 16

This two-storey townhouse is designed to be built on the north side of an east-west street, so that the street side faces south. Each unit requires a 6-m-wide lot and has 116 m² of floor area and a basement.

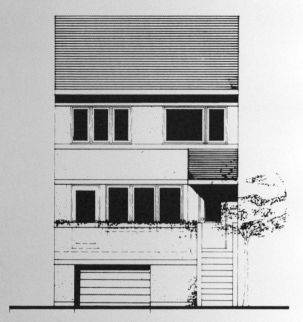

View from the street (south side of house)

This design provides for a sunken garage, with the rear portion extending into the basement of the house, and the front portion extending towards the street. The roof of this garage extension gives support for a deck that opens off the first-floor living room.

In addition to the living room and entry way, the first floor contains the dining room, kitchen and powder room. The floor plan is fairly open, with easy connection between individual spaces. There is a large pass-through in the wall separating the kitchen from the living room, and a partial-height wall separating the living room from the entry area. A doorway at the rear of the ground floor opens onto a rear deck. There are three bedrooms and a bathroom on the second floor.

Solar Features

The total glass-to-floor-area ratio 8.7 percent; and the south glass-to-floor-area ratio is 6.2 percent. The open design of the ground floor allows the sun to reach deep into the house. The pass-through, for example, admits direct light to the kitchen area. At the same time, the open design permits good cross-flow ventilation during the summer.

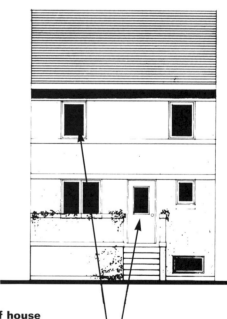

North side of house (single unit only)

Window area on north side of house is limited but still provides a sufficient area of openable window to ensure summertime cross-ventilation and natural lighting to rooms at rear

Access to rear deck is from the kitchen area

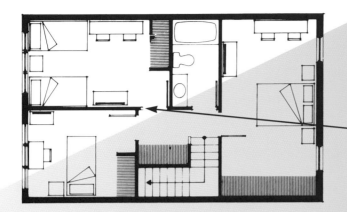

SECOND FLOOR

Note: Floor plan shown is for a single unit only. East and west walls are party walls shared with adjacent units

Elimination of the partition would provide for a single, large south-facing bedroom, with space for ensuite bathroom

As with many modern townhouses, the concrete used in the construction of the party walls between units, if plastered, can provide some storage of solar heat and help control overheating. This storage might be particularly beneficial on the second floor, where the depth of the house and the privacy requirements of bedrooms limit the distribution of solar gain by natural convection. Additional circulation of the solar gain by fans or other mechanical systems is proposed.

Location	Design For	Annual Heating (kW h/m²)	Solar Fraction
Vancouver	Gas Heat	53	0.55
	Electric Heat	26	0.67
Ottawa	Gas Heat	95	0.38
	Electric Heat	51	0.52
Winnipeg	Gas Heat	110	0.32
	Electric Heat	102	0.34

GROUND FLOOR

Pass-through assists in natural air circulation on the ground floor and admits sunlight to the kitchen area

Stairway provides access to basement and garage

MAIN ENTRANCE

0 1 2 3 4

M E T R E S

Design 17

This two-storey townhouse is designed for the south side of an east-west street, so that the rear of the house faces south. The design requires a 6-m-wide lot and has a floor area of 119 m² and a basement. As presented, it does not include a garage.

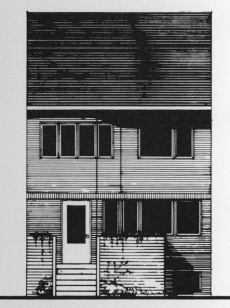

South side of house (single unit only)

Solar Features

The total glass-to-floor-area ratio is 7.5 percent; and the south glass-to-floor-area ratio is 5.3 percent. The large south-facing room on the ground floor and the open connection to the stairway and

Large overhang provides summer shading for some windows

Attached units can be built on both sides of the unit shown

View from the street (north side of house)

The house features a split entry, which allows the main entrance to be at ground level. The first-floor living area, which is five steps up from the entry hall, includes a kitchen with a breakfast area, a powder room and a large L-shaped living-and-dining-room combination. The living room portion of this space faces south and has a doorway onto the rear deck of the house. There are three bedrooms and a bathroom on the second floor. Two of the bedrooms are on the south side, where they receive a considerable amount of direct sunlight.

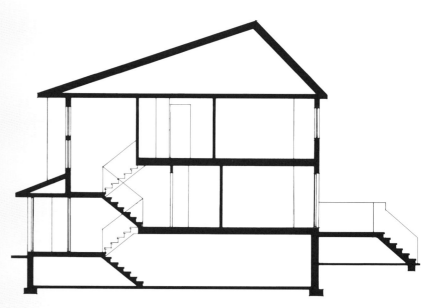

Section of house (looking from the east)

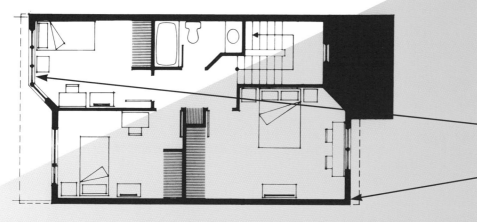

Broken line shows the extent of the south-facing roof overhang, which provides summertime shading to some of the windows

Window faces southeast, providing extra early morning solar gain

Walls between units are generally concrete and provide thermal mass for storage of solar gain

kitchen on the north side of the house allow for natural circulation.

On the second floor, circulation is more restricted. A mechanical system, such as a two-speed fan on the forced-air furnace would help reduce overheating. The angled window in the bedroom on the southwest side of the unit provides most of its solar gain in the morning when the house is heating up from a cold night. However, the other units in the row—those with the reverse floor plan—will receive this extra solar gain in the afternoon, typically at the time when the house does not need more solar input.

Location	Design For	Annual Heating (kW h/m²)	Solar Fraction
Vancouver	Gas Heat	49	0.35
	Electric Heat	26	0.46
Ottawa	Gas Heat	81	0.22
	Electric Heat	45	0.32
Winnipeg	Gas Heat	84	0.17
	Electric Heat	78	0.18

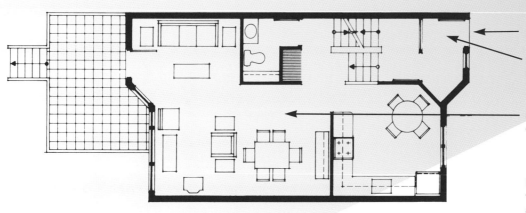

SECOND FLOOR

MAIN ENTRANCE

Entry area includes an air lock to reduce heat loss

Large room helps in the distribution of solar gain

Note: Floor plan shown is for a single unit only. East and west walls are party walls shared with adjacent units

0 1 2 3 4

M E T R E S

Design 18

This townhouse is designed for the south side of an east-west street, so that the rear of the house faces south. It can be built on a 5-m-wide lot. The house is a split-level, providing 104 m² of floor space, excluding the basement and garage.

and the rest on the upper level. The stairwell is built in an open design from the basement to the upper level of the second floor and beyond, rising to a clerestory window above the second-floor ceiling level.

South side of house (showing single unit only)

View from the street (north side of house)

The living areas of the house are on two floors, each divided into a lower and upper level. Downstairs from the first floor is a two-level basement-garage area, which also serves as the utility entrance to the house and provides space for a small powder room.

Many split-level townhouse designs have the main entrance at the garage level. This design locates it on the upper level of the first floor, providing increased convenience, reduced stair traffic and less sense of stratification of the home (which some buyers find undesirable).

The first-floor entry area connects directly to the dining room and the kitchen. The lower level of the first floor is entirely occupied by the living room, which opens onto a raised rear deck. The second floor includes three bedrooms and the main bathroom, with one bedroom on the lower level

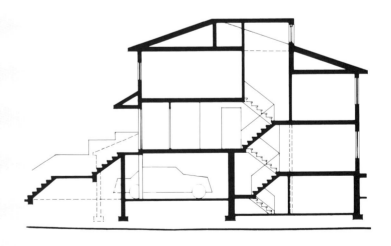

Section of house (looking from the west)

Rear deck has solid banister

102

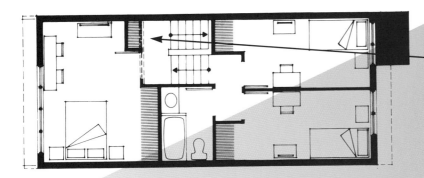

Stairwell receives direct
sunlight from clerestory
window above

Solar Features

The total glass-to-floor-area ratio is 9.4 percent;
and the south glass-to-floor-area ratio is 6.1 percent. The large glass areas in the living room and
bedroom and the south-facing clerestory generate
considerable solar gain. The open stairwell helps
the natural circulation of solar gain, but additional
circulation is necessary to prevent overheating.
The party walls between the units also help prevent overheating as they provide thermal mass
areas for the storage of excess solar gain.

Location	Design For	Annual Heating (kW h/m²)	Solar Fraction
Vancouver	Gas Heat	43	0.43
	Electric Heat	22	0.56
Ottawa	Gas Heat	77	0.29
	Electric Heat	40	0.41
Winnipeg	Gas Heat	81	0.22
	Electric Heat	73	0.24

FIRST FLOOR

Air lock entry reduces heat
loss at front door

MAIN ENTRANCE

An opening in the solid
kitchen wall could be
provided to allow views into
the living room, increased
sunlight to the kitchen and
improved air circulation

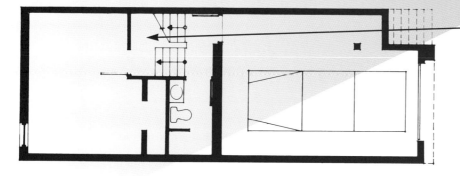

BASEMENT

Utility entrance provides
direct access from the
garage to the living areas
of the house

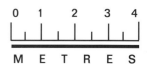

```
0   1   2   3   4
|_|_|_|_|_|_|_|_|
M  E  T  R  E  S
```

Design 19

This two-storey townhouse was designed to be built on the north side of an east-west street, so that the front of the house faces south. Each individual unit requires a 4.3-m-wide lot. The design provides 110 m² of floor space on the two main

Solar Features

Although the south-facing side of the house is small in area, the design provides a considerable area of south-facing glass. The total glass-to-floor-

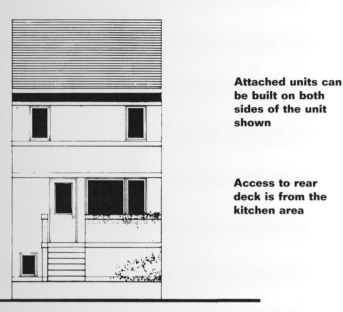

North side of house (showing single unit only)

Attached units can be built on both sides of the unit shown

Access to rear deck is from the kitchen area

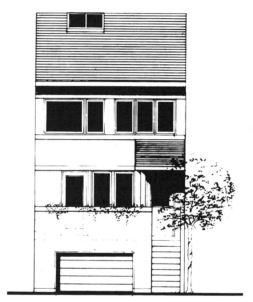

View from the street (south side of house)

levels plus a basement. It also provides for a sunken garage, the back of which extends into the basement space, and the front of which protrudes towards the street. The roof of this extended garage serves as support for a deck opening off the kitchen on the first floor of the house.

The kitchen, living room and dining room are located on the first floor. The layout is open, with few dividing walls. A door opens off the living room to the rear yard and deck.

On the second floor, there are three bedrooms and a bathroom. In addition, a central portion of the second floor is open, looking down onto the dining room and up to a skylight on the roof above.

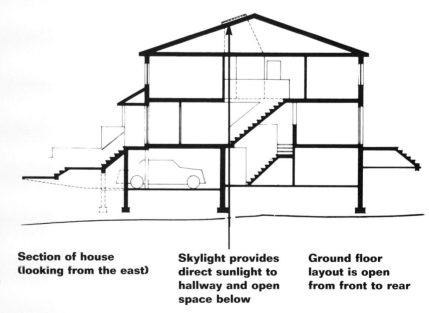

Section of house (looking from the east)

Skylight provides direct sunlight to hallway and open space below

Ground floor layout is open from front to rear

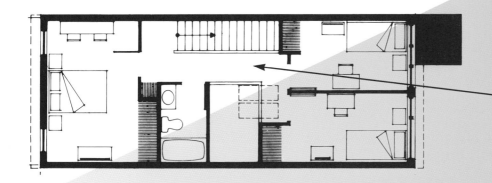

Skylights above require summertime shading

Hallway overlooks dining room below

area ratio is 7.5 percent; and the south glass-to-floor-area ratio is 5.3 percent. The house design allows sunlight and solar heat to reach deep into the house structure. The open layout of the ground floor and the open space rising above the dining room to the skylight are both beneficial.

As in most townhouses, the mass in the party wall between the units helps to provide storage of solar gain. During the summer, the design allows for good cross-ventilation. However, without blinds or other shading devices, the skylight will provide excessive solar gain at certain times of the year.

Location	Design For	Annual Heating (kW h/m²)	Solar Fraction
Vancouver	Gas Heat	40	0.40
	Electric Heat	26	0.49
Ottawa	Gas Heat	65	0.29
	Electric Heat	40	0.28
Winnipeg	Gas Heat	77	0.21
	Electric Heat	73	0.22

GROUND FLOOR

MAIN ENTRANCE

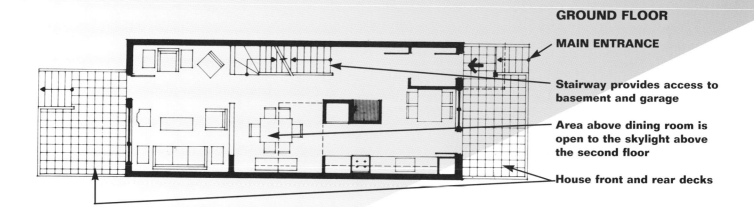

Stairway provides access to basement and garage

Area above dining room is open to the skylight above the second floor

House front and rear decks

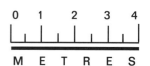

0 1 2 3 4

M E T R E S

Design 20

This three-storey townhouse is designed for the north side of an east-west street, so that the front of the house faces south. Each unit requires a 4.25-m-wide lot. The house has 118 m² of floor includes two bedrooms, both of which have dormers on the north side. In addition, the third floor includes a large open area overlooking the second floor below (and the ground-floor dining

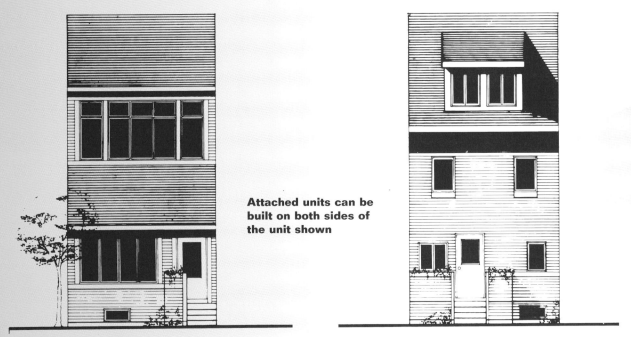

View from the street (south side of house)

Attached units can be built on both sides of the unit shown

North side of house (single unit only)

area and a full basement. As presented, the design does not include a garage.

This house offers several unusual features. The ground floor, which is the largest, extends forward from the front of the second and third stories. The design has a deep living-dining-room combination, served by a large area of south-facing windows. An irregularly shaped space above the dining room is open through both floors, rising to a ceiling at the top of the house some 5 m above eye level. At the rear of the second floor, a powder room, kitchen and breakfast nook open onto a rear deck.

The second floor features a single large bedroom in the rear and the main bathroom. The hallway of the second floor overlooks the dining room below. The third floor

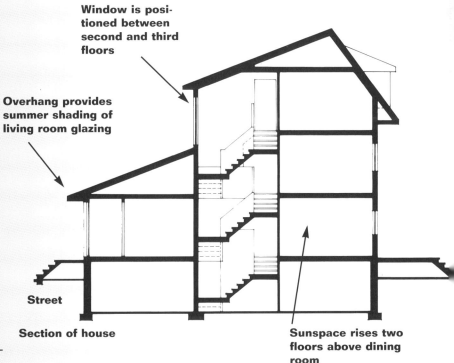

Window is positioned between second and third floors

Overhang provides summer shading of living room glazing

Street

Section of house

Sunspace rises two floors above dining room

106

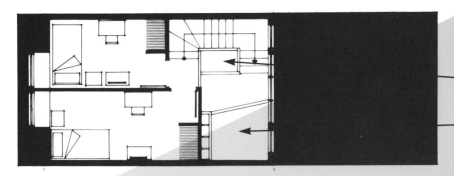

THIRD FLOOR

Dormers provide sunlight to bedrooms

Stairwell is open down to basement

Open sunspace looks down on second floor hallway and ground-floor dining room

room through the smaller open area in the second floor).

Solar Features

The total glass-to-floor-area ratio is 11.8 percent; and the south glass-to-floor-area ratio is 8.4 percent. The glass is arranged mainly in two large groupings. The first area of glass is in the living room, where it provides light and solar gain deep into the house. The second large block of glass is located on the south-facing wall adjacent to the open space between the second and third floors. The windows, which extend virtually the full width of the building and are nearly a storey in height, provide direct light and solar gain to the stairway, to the hallways on the second and third floors, and to the dining area in the middle of the ground floor.

In addition to allowing sunshine to reach many parts of the house, the open design encourages natural air circulation. Additional circulation by means of the furnace fan helps to prevent overheating.

Location	Design For	Annual Heating (kW h/m²)	Solar Fraction
Vancouver	Gas Heat	38	0.50
	Electric Heat	19	0.64
Ottawa	Gas Heat	68	0.35
	Electric Heat	37	0.47
Winnipeg	Gas Heat	75	0.27
	Electric Heat	70	0.29

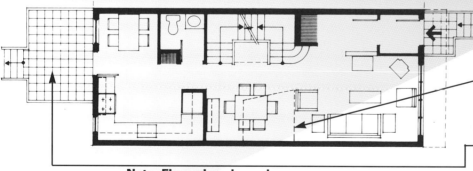

SECOND FLOOR

Glazed and sloping ceiling provides light into the second-floor bathroom

Hallway provides bridge effect between stairwell on one side and open space on the other

Space is open down to dining room below

GROUND FLOOR

Front entrance includes an air lock entry to reduce heat loss

Open connection between living room and dining area provides bright sunshine and helps with air circulation

Rear deck opens off breakfast nook

Note: Floor plan shown is for a single unit only. East and west walls are party walls shared with adjacent units

0 1 2 3 4

METRES

SOLAR ALTITUDE AND AZIMUTH ANGLES

Date	Time AM	Time PM	Solar Position 43°N Latitude ALT	AZIMUTH	Solar Position 45°N Latitude ALT	AZIMUTH	Solar Position 47°N Latitude ALT	AZIMUTH
December 21	8	4	3.7	52.8	2.5	52.7	1.2	52.6
	9	3	11.7	41.5	10.7	41.2	8.7	41.0
	10	2	18.0	28.8	16.3	28.5	14.5	28.5
	11	1	22.1	14.9	20.2	14.7	18.3	14.5
	12	12	23.6	0.0	21.6	0.0	19.6	0.0
March 21	7	5	10.9	79.6	10.5	79.3	10.2	78.9
	8	4	21.4	68.5	20.7	67.8	19.9	67.1
	9	3	31.1	55.7	30.0	54.7	28.8	53.8
	10	2	39.3	40.2	37.8	39.2	36.2	38.2
	11	1	44.9	21.4	43.1	20.8	41.2	20.1
	12	12	47.0	0.0	45.0	0.0	43.0	0.0
June 21	5	7	5.6	117.1	6.5	116.9	7.4	116.7
	6	6	15.7	107.6	16.3	107.1	16.9	106.5
	7	5	26.4	98.3	26.7	97.3	26.9	96.3
	8	9	37.4	88.4	37.3	86.9	37.1	85.4
	9	3	48.2	76.9	47.7	74.7	47.2	72.6
	10	2	58.5	61.3	57.5	58.6	56.4	56.0
	11	1	66.9	37.2	65.2	34.5	63.6	32.2
	12	12	70.4	0.0	68.4	0.0	66.4	0.0
September 21	7	5	10.9	79.6	10.5	79.3	10.2	78.9
	8	4	21.4	68.5	20.7	67.8	19.9	67.1
	9	3	31.1	55.7	30.0	54.7	28.8	53.8
	10	2	39.3	40.2	37.8	39.2	36.2	38.3
	11	1	44.9	21.4	43.1	20.8	41.2	20.1
	12	12	47.0	0.0	45.0	0.0	43.0	0.0

Date	Time AM	Time PM	Solar Position 49°N Latitude ALT	AZIMUTH	Solar Position 51°N Latitude ALT	AZIMUTH	Solar Position 53°N Latitude ALT	AZIMUTH
December 21	9	3	7.2	40.8	5.7	40.7	4.2	40.6
	10	2	12.8	28.1	11.0	27.9	9.2	27.7
	11	1	16.3	14.3	14.4	14.2	12.4	14.1
	12	12	17.6	0.0	15.0	0.0	13.6	0.0
March 21	7	5	9.8	78.6	9.4	78.2	9.0	77.9
	8	4	19.1	66.5	18.3	65.8	17.5	65.2
	9	3	27.6	53.0	26.4	52.1	25.2	51.4
	10	2	34.6	37.4	33.0	36.6	31.4	35.9
	11	1	39.3	19.5	37.4	19.0	35.5	18.5
	12	12	41.0	0.0	39.0	0.0	37.0	0.0
June 21	4	8			1.2	127.4	2.4	127.3
	5	7	8.3	116.4	9.2	116.1	10.1	115.8
	6	6	17.5	105.9	18.0	105.3	18.5	104.6
	7	5	27.1	95.3	27.3	94.3	27.4	93.2
	8	4	37.0	83.9	36.7	82.4	36.4	80.9
	9	3	46.5	70.6	45.8	68.6	45.1	66.8
	10	2	55.2	53.6	54.0	51.3	52.7	49.3
	11	1	61.8	30.2	60.1	28.4	58.3	26.9
	12	12	64.4	0.0	62.4	0.0	60.4	0.0
September 21	7	5	9.8	78.6	9.4	78.2	9.0	77.9
	8	4	19.1	66.5	18.3	66.5	17.5	65.2
	9	3	27.6	53.0	26.4	52.1	25.2	51.4
	10	2	34.6	37.4	13.0	36.6	31.4	35.9
	11	1	39.3	19.5	37.4	19.0	35.5	18.5
	12	12	41.0	0.0	19.0	0.0	37.0	0.0

System Requirements

- Microsoft Windows 3.1, 3.11 or Windows 95
- Microsoft Excel, Version 5.0 or later
- Windows-compatible printer capable of printing in landscape mode

Display:

- standard VGA (640 x 480); requires vertical scrolling for input and horizontal scrolling to see out puts and recommendations (unless VIEW ZOOM set to about 75%)
- super VGA (800 x 600); requires vertical scrolling for input and some horizontal scrolling to see outputs and recommendations (unless VIEW ZOOM set to about 85%)
- super VGA (1168 x 768) or higher; requires vertical scrolling for input

Who Should Use This Software?

The *Comfort Design Checker* software provides guidelines to designers of single detached and attached residences that have southern, southeastern and soutwestern exposures.

With this software, you can check the house design for excessive solar overheating in the winter. Guidelines are provided for recommended window areas, shading, internal utilities consumption and thermal storage mass for houses at various levels of conservation.

Use this modelling tool at the Conceptual stage of design. Other, more detailed simulation software is available for use at the Sketch and Detailed Design stages to refine the design, determine energy usage, and so on.

Installation of Software

Copy the spreadsheet file **SOLARCK.xls** into a directory on your hard drive, or run the program from a floppy diskette. (Remember to make a backup copy of the file.)

From Windows, click **FILE**, then **OPEN** on the menu bar to load **EXCEL** and load the file **SOLARCK.xls** from the drive and directory to which you copied it.

Click on the tab labelled **Solar Check** at the bottom of the sheet.

Program Layout

The spreadsheet workbook **SOLARCK.xls** contains four sheets, accessed by tabs at the bottom:

- **HELP** — a description of inputs, output and recommendations.
- **Solar Check** — input and output for the overheating design checker. This sheet is protected. You can enter data only in the boxes.
- **Parametrics** — a lookup table of recommended south glazing; it is used in the Solar Check sheet. This sheet is protected. You can not enter data.
- **Weather** — data for 68 Canadian cities; it is used in the Solar Check sheet. This sheet is protected. You can enter data only in the rows labelled "user defined."

Getting Ready

You need to enter the following information into the *Comfort Design Checker* (note: you can experiment with different values for any of these inputs):

- location (city, province)
- main and basement floor areas
- window areas (by orientation, main and heated basement)
- predominant window types—number of glazings, number of low-E coatings (by orientation)
- approximate percentage of internal and external shading
- predominant overhang dimensions (for south windows)
- general thermal storage mass characteristics of the house
- general conservation level of the house
- mechanical system characteristics:
  - mechanical cooling?
  - forced air heating?
- general level of efficiency of applicances and lighting
- thermostat setpoints

ENTERING DATA

- Click on the Solar Check tab at the bottom of the sheet.
- On the Solar Check sheet, make your entries only in the boxes. (The other cells are protected from user input.)

As you enter the values, the outputs and recommendations on the right-hand side are updated.

Enter the information as follows:

Run ID...	Enter the house identification.
Description...	Enter the house description.
1. Location	Enter the location number. (See list of city numbers in Weather sheet.)

2. House Description

Detached/Attached?	Enter **D** for detached housing or **A** for duplex or row housing (results are approximate for latter).
Main and upper floor area	Enter the heated floor area in square metres.
Basement heated?	Enter **Y** for heated or **N** for unheated. (If you enter **N**, this will not be included in the calculations.)
Basement floor area	Enter the heated basement floor area in square metres.

3. South Windows

Main and upper window area	Enter the south window area in square metres.
Basement window area	Enter the south basement window area in square metres.

Type

No. of glazings	Enter the predominant number of glazings.
No. of low-E coatings	Enter the predominant number of low-E coatings.
Shading by curtains	Consider the winter shading by curtains and blinds (including usage). If unknown, use a range of 5-15%.
October to April shading	Estimate the winter external shading caused by buildings and trees to the south using one of the following methods (in descending order of preference).

1) Standing on the site near the centre of the spot where the major south glazings will be located, plot obstructions on a sun-path chart (such as "Sun Angles For Design" by Robert Bennet) using a clinometer and compass. Estimate the amount of shading between 45° east and west of south and below the vertical angle shown for October.

2) Standing on the site near the centre of the spot where the major glazings will be located, estimate the amount of shading between approximately 45° east and west of south and below the estimated vertical angle shown for October in the print-out of the program.

Shading (south windows)

Window overhang	Enter the most common overhang dimensions in metres. The window overhang determines the lookup value to be used in the Parametric sheet (based on an overhang of 0.6 m, 0.9 m or 1.2 m).
Eave-to-glass distance Average glass height	Eave-to-glass distance and glass height are compared to base values to calculate a modifier to the values from the Parametric sheet.
Window area with overhang	Enter the percentage of south window area with overhang dimensions shown. If less than 50%, the recommended glazed area will be based on a lesser overhang (1.2 m changed to 0.9 m, 0.9 m to 0.6 m).

4. East and West Windows

East area   Enter the east window area in square metres.

West area   Enter the west window area in square metres.

Type and Shading

East/west no. of panes   Enter predominant number of panes.

No. of low-E coatings   Enter predominant number of low-E coatings.

Tinting/shading   Estimate winter shading by tinting, curtains and blinds (including usage). If unknown, use an average of 5-15% for curtains and blinds.

Fall/spring shading
- to the east
- to the west

Estimate the winter external shading by buildings, and to the east and west, using one of the following methods (in descending order of preference).

1) Standing on the site near the centre of the spot where the major east and west glazings will be located, plot obstructions on a sun-path chart (such as "Sun Angles For Design" by Robert Bennet) using a clinometer and compass. Estimate the amount of shading between 45° north and south of east and below the vertical angle shown for 30°. Repeat for west.

2) Standing on the site near the centre of the spot where the major glazings will be located, estimate the amount of shading between approximately 45° north and south and below an estimated vertical angle of 30°. Repeat for west.

5. Mass

Extra mass   Enter **1** for wood-frame/gyproc construction.

Enter **2** for wood-frame/double gyproc construction.

Enter **3** for construction that includes double gyproc and about 6 to 8 times the south glazed area in masonry (mostly in direct sun) — brick, stone, concrete walls, concrete topcoat on floor with tile (preferably clay tile).

6. Insulation/Airtightness:

Conservation level   Enter **1** for normal insulation levels.

Enter **2** for R-2000 houses.

Enter **3** for Advanced houses (energy use is about half that of R-2000 houses).

7. Mechanical Systems

Cooling system

Enter **1** for none.

Enter **2** if mechanical cooling is planned.

A higher glazed area and more overheating can be acceptable if mechanical cooling is available to counteract the solar overheating. However, this would increase energy use. For example, if glazed areas were increased to a point where 7% of October hours were overheating hours, then 3% of October hours (abovethe 4% acceptable limit) would require mechanical cooling. In addition, above about 8% overheating hours in October, there will be excessive overheating in March and April (depending onthe house configuration, overhangs, and so on).

Heating distribution

Enter **1** for forced air.

Enter **2** for baseboard, radiant floor or radiant ceiling heating.

With **2**, because there is no forced air system to distribute heat gains from south to north rooms, enter the percentage of thermal storage in south rooms. The system uses this value and the floor area to determine the available thermal storage (and the recommended south window area).

8. Occupancy

Appliance and lighting efficiency

Enter **1** for conventional appliances and lights.

Enter **2** for medium-efficiency appliances and some fluorescent lighting.

Enter **3** for high-efficiency appliances and mostly fluorescent lighting.

Thermostat setpoints

Enter day and night heating setpoints — 21°C and 18°C, respectively. (Some temperature swing is necessary for effective use of thermal storage.) At high levels of conservation, this has a small effect because there is little temperature swing in an energy-efficient house.

INTERPRETING THE RESULTS

Design Optimization

As you enter values, the system updates outputs and recommendations on the right. (Some scrolling will be required for lower resolution displays.)

The primary output is the recommended maximum south window area (as an area and as a percentage of the heated floor area). The system also generates an estimate of the hours of overheating (in October). The recommendations are based on the assumption that overheating should be limited to 4 percent of the hours in order to maintain an acceptable level of comfort . The recommended maximum window area is based on the total heated floor area, without consideration of the window distribution.

However, the distribution of windows is important. Too large a proportion of windows in one area can result in excessive overheating. For example, if a heated basement is specified, its area is included in the total. If the basement has a very small window area, the total window area may be less than the maximum recommended. However, the window areas on the main and second floors could cause excessive overheating on those floors.

The purpose of the *Comfort Design Checker* software is to enable the designer to formulate a design "package" that provides a comfortable environment for the occupants. As a general guide, the following changes result in greater recommended south window area:

- increased floor area;
- higher performance glazing (more glazings, more low-E coatings);
- increased shading by curtains or blinds, but particularly by external shading. This also results in increased energy use;
- increased seasonally selective shading by
  – increasing the size of the overhang
  – reducing the eave-to-glass distance
  – reducing the glass height;
- more thermal storage mass (see Figure 2.16 in Chapter 8);
- reduced level of conservation (see Figure 2.13 and Table 2.6 in Chapter 8);
- use of forced air distribution;
- more efficient appliances and lighting; and
- use of a thermostat setback (particularly with normal conservation levels).

Limitations of the *Comfort Design Checker* Software

There are two main types of errors associated with the results:

- errors associated with Suncode hourly simulations; and
- errors associated with simplifications in deriving the "rules of thumb" in Table 2.2 from the simulation results. These were within 2 percent of the predicted hours of overheating in 81 percent of the cases. This amounts to a difference in recommended south glazed area of less than 0.5 percent of the heated floor area.

Additional errors can occur if the *Comfort Design Checker* software is used for conditions outside the range of conditions in the original simulations. The simulations were performed for five cities across Canada with latitudes ranging from 43.7° to 53.6° latitude. This range covers most of the major population centres in Canada.

The software guidelines apply only to overheating during the heating season in a heating-dominant climate. Overheating during the summer would have to be taken care of using external shading, venting or mechanical cooling.

The results apply to single detached houses. The results for attached housing are approximated by assuming the next highest conservation level.

The software predicted slightly higher hours of overheating than measured for the monitored houses but successfully predicted excessive overheating in most cases.